BOOKS BY JULES FEIFFER

Sick, Sick, Sick
Passionella
The Explainers
Boy, Girl Boy, Girl
Hold Me!
Harry, the Rat with Women
Feiffer's Album
*The Unexpurgated Memoirs
    of Bernard Mergendeiler*
The Great Comic Book Heroes
Feiffer on Civil Rights
Feiffer's Marriage Manual

Little Murders

LITTLE MURDERS

JULES FEIFFER

Random House · New York

Third Printing

Library of Congress Catalog Card Number: 67–25077

Manufactured in the United States of America

28th April 1967.

Dear Sir,

"Little Murders"

  I am desired by the Lord Chamberlain to inform
you that he regrets he must disallow from the above-
named play those parts detailed in the annexure to
this letter. An undertaking that these disallowances
will be observed must be submitted before a licence
for the play can be issued.

  Should you wish to make any substitutions these
should be submitted for approval by the Lord
Chamberlain before they can be included in the manu-
script.

       Yours faithfully,

       Assistant Comptroller.

Jeremy Brooks, Esq.

LORD CHAMBERLAIN'S OFFICE,

ST JAMES'S PALACE, S.W.I.

Appendix to letter to Mr. J. Brooks
dated 28th April 1967

LITTLE MURDERS

The Lord Chamberlain disallows the following parts of the stage-play:

Act I-1-20: '..shit..' (3 times)

   I-3-34: From 'I married a musician last year...to & inclusive of '...it turned out all right.'

   I-3-36: '..meaning, I suppose, you won't cut his balls off. Yet some men like that.'

   2-1-3: '..shit.'

   2-1-4: 'shit.' (5 times)

   2-2-11: '..shit..'

   2-2-26: '..shit..' (3 times)

Little Murders

"Two, four, six, eight—who do we assassinate?"

—New York children's
street chant,
circa 1964

CAST OF CHARACTERS

Marjorie Newquist
Kenny Newquist
Carol Newquist
Patsy Newquist
Alfred Chamberlain
Judge Stern
Reverend Dupas
Assorted Wedding Guests
Lieutenant Practice

SYNOPSIS OF SCENES

Act One

Scene 1: The Newquist apartment
Scene 2: The Newquist apartment, one month later
Scene 3: The Newquist apartment, two months later

Act Two

Scene 1: The Newquist apartment, four hours later
Scene 2: The Newquist apartment, six months later

Act One

A view of the Newquist apartment. The living room, din-
ing area, foyer and front door slowly fade into view (by
means of a scrim or any other workable method), in sync
with the rising sound of city street noises. The apartment
is typically Upper West Side, dominated by overstuffed
furniture, enormous multipaned windows and walls with
too much molding. At the moment, mid-morning, it is
empty. As the apartment fades into view the level of noise
rises—morning noise: construction, traffic and helicopters.
In the next few minutes both light and noise change:
shadows shift, lengthen and darken in sync with the fad-
ing of construction sounds, replaced by the late afternoon
cries of children at play. This too fades into the quieter
monotone of early evening traffic.

The apartment darkens accordingly and we may even
see the setting sun as reflected in the apartment windows
across the street. (The only view of the world outside is of
other buildings, other windows.) What we see is comparable
to a stop-motion camera's view of the apartment, from mid-
morning to dusk. Throughout, a steady patina of soot has
drifted in through one of the half-open windows, and specks
of plaster may now and then drop from the ceiling. The
telephone rings. Other sounds: police sirens, fire engines,
etc. The front door unlocks; this takes time, since there are

two double locks on the door. The door slowly pushes open, revealing two enormous shopping bags. Almost completely hidden behind them is MARJORIE, *small, energetic, in her fifties. She switches on the foyer light with an elbow and bustles across to the kitchen.*

MARJORIE Don't let a draft in! (*As she disappears through the swinging door that leads to the kitchen,* KENNY *enters reading a paperback. He is listless, in his early twenties. Leaving the door open he starts slowly across the room, engrossed in his reading. On the return swing of the kitchen door,* MARJORIE *reappears sans coat and shopping bags, this time carrying a folded tablecloth and a large sponge*) I'm going to need your help, young man. (KENNY *enters bathroom, closes door loudly*) Don't dawdle! (MARJORIE *runs sponge across dining-room table. It comes up pitch black*) Filth! (*She unfolds tablecloth in one motion. It falls perfectly into place*) They'll be here any minute, Kenny!

> (*She disappears into kitchen with sponge, reappears on return swing of door with serving cart piled high with dishes and silver. She is about to set table when an explosion of automobile horns drives her to window, which she slams shut with great effort. She hastens to other window and switches on air conditioner—a loud hum.* CAROL *enters, carrying brief case. He is a short, thickset, energetic man in his fifties, about* MARJORIE's *size*)

CAROL What the hell is that for? This is February!
(*Switches off air conditioner*)

MARJORIE (*A cheerful but uninterested hug*) It drowns out the traffic.

CAROL (*Slips out of embrace*) All right, when we don't have guests. We don't want people to think we're crazy. Did the liquor come?

MARJORIE It came. (*Suspicious*) Why are you so interested in liquor?

CAROL Don't worry. You've got nothing to worry about.

MARJORIE You called up twice from the office to ask about the liquor.

CAROL That's all right. That's perfectly all right. (*Evades her stare*) You can find out a lot more about somebody, you know, when he's a little—
(*He flutters his hand to indicate tippsiness*)

MARJORIE (*Shocked*) Carol, you're not going to get that poor boy *drunk!*

CAROL That poor boy wants to marry my Patsy! And don't call me *Carol!*
(*Sounds of toilet flush and door slam.* KENNY *enters from bathroom, reading*)

MARJORIE But—dear—you haven't even met him!

KENNY (*Matter-of-fact*) He's an artsy-fartsy photographer. Patsy says he's thirty-six, but I know he's forty.

CAROL (*To* KENNY) Are you *reading* again? (*He grabs paperback*) *Harlots of Venus!* Is that what I spend seven thousand a year on graduate school for? Get dressed!

KENNY You lost my place!
(KENNY *exits*)

CAROL Why is she doing this to me?

MARJORIE He'll be a fine boy. I know it in my bones.

CAROL What are you talking about? Do you have the slightest idea what you're talking about? She's only known him three weeks! I bet he's a fag!

MARJORIE Carol!

CAROL (*Vicious*) I *hate* that name! I told you never to call me that name. You deliberately do that to annoy me! (*Shouts*) Call me *dear!* (*Subsides*) You refuse to look at the facts. This whole family. That's the trouble with it. I'm the only one who looks at the facts. What was the name of that interior decorator she went to Europe with?

MARJORIE Howard. He was—delicate.

CAROL Swish! And that *actor,* the one who she went camping up in Maine with?

MARJORIE Roger. He was very muscular.

CAROL Swish! And the musician. And the stockbroker. And the Jewish novelist!

MARJORIE Oh, *they're* not like that—

CAROL Swish! Swish! Swish! I can spot 'em a mile away. She draws 'em like flies. Too strong for real men. Too much stuff! (*Proudly*) She's got *too much stuff!* Wait, you'll see. This new one—what's his name?

MARJORIE Alfred.

CAROL A swish name if I ever heard one. You'll see. He'll come in. Be very polite. Very charming. Look handsome. Well dressed. Have a strong handshake. Look me right in the eye. Smile a lot. Have white teeth. Shiny hair. Look very regular. But after two or three drinks—look at his wrists—he'll have trouble keeping 'em straight. Watch his lips. He'll start smacking his lips with his tongue. Watch his eyes. He'll start rolling his eyes. And his legs will go from being crossed like this—(*Wide-legged*) to this (*Close-legged*). And when he gets up to start walking—(*He is about to mimic walk. Offstage sound of shots.* CAROL *and* MARJORIE *rush to window. He struggles, but can't get it open*) Damn! Goddamn!

MARJORIE Hurry! (*Shots fade. Offstage siren, loud, then fading*) They're miles away by now. You take forever. (*Doorbell*)

PATSY'S VOICE Hey, everybody!
>   (CAROL *outpaces* MARJORIE *to door.* PATSY *and* ALFRED *enter. Much excitement, laughter.* CAROL *is more involved with his daughter than* MARJORIE, *who is just a touch restrained.* PATSY *is all-consuming. Tall, blond, vibrant, the All-American Girl.* ALFRED *is big, heavyset and quite dour. He is in his middle thirties. Two cameras hang from straps around his neck.* PATSY, MARJORIE *and* CAROL *speak in unison. None of the following is intelligible*)

PATSY Daddy, Mother, I love your hair! Daddy, you're putting on weight, Mother, Daddy.

MARJORIE Hello, dear, how are you, what's wrong with my hair, you're putting on weight.

CAROL Patsy, Patsy, my little girl! My baby girl, you look like a million dollars! I'll tell the world.

PATSY This is Alfred!

CAROL (*Ignoring* ALFRED, *to* PATSY) Hey, you weren't in that business down there?

PATSY What business?

CAROL   Well, from now on just be more careful.

MARJORIE (*Her eyes on* ALFRED)   I don't think we need worry any longer, dear. Patsy's finally got herself a *man!*
(CAROL *scowls*)

PATSY   Where's my Kenny?
(*Offstage sound of toilet flush and door slam.* KENNY *enters, adjusting trousers.* PATSY *swoops down on him.* PATSY *and* KENNY *speak in unison. None of the following is intelligible*)

PATSY   Kenny! My baby brother! Isn't he the absolute cutest? I could eat him alive! Kenny!

KENNY   Ah, come on, cut it out! Quit all the hugging! Quit it! Boy, oboy, oboy.

MARJORIE (*Somewhat catty*)   Alfred, have you ever seen such a madhouse?
(ALFRED *smiles diffidently*)

CAROL   He's in the house for three minutes and she's already putting him on the spot. Have you ever seen anything like it, Alfred?
(ALFRED *smiles diffidently*)

PATSY   Kenny! You're so handsome! I can't get over it! (*To* ALFRED) I've always had a mad thing on my kid brother! (KENNY *clowns embarrassment,* PATSY *and* MAR-

JORIE *laugh*, ALFRED *smiles diffidently*, CAROL *looks annoyed. To* ALFRED) He breaks me up!

CAROL (*Nastily*) Kenny's the *comedian* around here. (KENNY *sobers immediately. To* ALFRED) What's your pleasure, young fellow?

PATSY Mother, what have you done to this room?
(*Lights flicker and black out in apartment, and in windows across the street*)

MARJORIE (*Lighting candles*) Nothing special. A little bit of this. A little bit of that.
(*Offstage sirens begin*)

CAROL (*Self-pityingly*) If you bothered to come here more often—

MARJORIE (*Studying* PATSY's *face by candlelight*) I don't like your looks.

CAROL (*Studying* PATSY) What's the matter? The day that girl doesn't look like a million dollars—

MARJORIE You've got black rings under your eyes.

PATSY Mother, that's eyeliner.

MARJORIE Makes you look exhausted.

KENNY (*Studying* PATSY)   I like it.

MARJORIE   Always together!

CAROL   Do you have the slightest idea what you're talking about? She looks like a million dollars!

MARJORIE   I know. It's what they're wearing today. I'm out of step. As usual.
(*Lights come back on.* MARJORIE *blows out candle*)

CAROL (*A little nervous. To* ALFRED)   What's your pleasure, young fellow?

MARJORIE (*Critical*)   Why don't you wear your other out-fit?

PATSY   What other outfit?

CAROL   Will you stop criticizing?

PATSY   What other outfit, Mother?

MARJORIE   I can't be expected to remember everything. It's not as if you still lived here.

KENNY   Hey, Al, want to see Patsy's old room?

PATSY   *Alfred*, Kenny. And he's not interested in that!

KENNY   I bet he is! Want to?

ALFRED   Maybe later.

KENNY (*Rejected*)   Why should I care?

CAROL (*To* KENNY)   He doesn't want to! Stop acting silly! (*To* ALFRED) What's your pleasure, young fellow?

MARJORIE   Alfred, may I shake your hand? My mother taught us that you could tell a lot about a person by the way he shakes hands. (*Shakes his hand*) You have a good hand. (*Flirtatious*) Better look out, Patsy! I'll steal your boy friend! (*Releases* ALFRED's *hand. Short laugh. To* ALFRED) I'm only joking.

KENNY   Let me try. (*Shakes* ALFRED's *hand*) You don't squeeze so hard. (*Disengages*) Dad?

CAROL   This is the silliest business I've ever heard of! I think we all need drinks. What's your pleasure, young fellow?

MARJORIE   Alfred, is something the matter with your face?

ALFRED (*To* PATSY)   Is there?

PATSY (*Subdued annoyance*)   Just the usual assortment of bruises, Mother.

MARJORIE   What kind of talk is that? Modern talk?

PATSY (*Not overjoyed to be on the subject*) Alfred is always getting beat up, Mother. At least once a week. (*To* ALFRED) Or is it more?

ALFRED (*Shakes his head to indicate it is not more*) I don't get hurt.

MARJORIE You don't get hurt? Carol, look at that boy! His face is a mass of bruises!

CAROL I have asked you repeatedly never to call me Carol. (*To* PATSY) I hate that name Carol!

MARJORIE I have to call you something, dear.

CAROL I don't care what you call me. Just don't call me Carol!

KENNY Call him Harriet! (*Laughs*) Harriet! Harriet! *Yoohoo!* Harriet!
    (*Convulses himself*)

PATSY You're not being funny, Kenny. (*He sobers immediately*) I love your name. I know lots of men named Carol.

KENNY Sure. Sure. Name one.
    (CAROL *glares at him*)

PATSY (*Thinking*) Carol—

KENNY *Chessman!*
(*Screams with laughter*)

PATSY King Carol of Rumania!

CAROL That's right! King Carol! Damn it, that's right! Say, I feel like a drink. Anyone join me?

MARJORIE I want to know why Alfred gets into these fights. I don't think that's the least bit funny.

PATSY (*Resigned*) Ask him!

ALFRED (*Not interested but making an effort, mindful that this is his first attempt at conversation*) Look. (*Long pause. Others stir uncomfortably*) There are lots of little people who like to start fights with big people. They hit me for a couple of minutes, they see I'm not going to fall down, they get tired and they go away.

MARJORIE (*After an embarrassed pause*) So much tension. Rush. Rush. Rush. My mother taught me to take dainty, little steps. She'd *kill* me if she saw the stride on Patsy.

CAROL (*Puzzled. The beginnings of contempt*) Don't you defend yourself?

ALFRED I ask them not to hit my cameras. They're quite good about that. (*Cheerful*) Surprising!

CAROL   Let me get this straight. You just stand there and let these hooligans do whatever they want to you?

ALFRED   I'm quite strong, so you needn't worry about it. At the risk of sounding arrogant, this has been going on for ten years and I've yet to be knocked unconscious.

CAROL   But why don't you fight back?

ALFRED   I don't want to.

CAROL   Christ Jesus, you're not a pacifist?

PATSY *(Warning)*   Daddy—

ALFRED *(Slowly shakes his head)*   An apathist. *(Blank stares from* CAROL *and* MARJORIE*)* I want to do what I want to do, not what *they* want me to do.

CAROL   So you just stand there.

ALFRED   It doesn't hurt.

CAROL   Getting your face beat in doesn't hurt?

ALFRED   Not if you daydream. I daydream all through it. About my work. I imagine myself standing there, in the same spot, clicking off roll after roll of film, humming to myself with pleasure. I hum to myself when I work.

There are times when I get so carried away that I think I'm actually doing what I'm only dreaming I'm doing. Muggers tend to get very depressed when you hum all the while they're hitting you. It's not something I choose to happen. It's just one of those things you learn to live with.

PATSY (*To family*) Look, this is an old argument and it doesn't really concern you. Why don't we get on something else?

CAROL (*Indignant*) It certainly does concern me, young lady!

PATSY (*Placating*) Oh, Daddy—

CAROL I want you to know it concerns me very much. (*To* ALFRED) How do you get into these things? You must do something to get them mad—

ALFRED No—

CAROL Well, Goddamnit, you're getting *me* mad!

MARJORIE (*Taking the heat off*) Alfred, do you try *talking* to them?

ALFRED (*The patient old pro*) There's no way of talking someone out of beating you up if that's what he wants to do.

KENNY (*To* PATSY) This guy's a riot!
   (*She slaps at him. He playfully eludes her*)

PATSY Haven't we had enough of this? I'm going to make some drinks.

KENNY Vodka and tonic.

MARJORIE Just *one*, young man.

CAROL I'll make them!

PATSY No, Daddy. I want to get my hands busy. Alfred?

ALFRED Nothing right now.

CAROL You don't drink either. Is that right?

ALFRED I drink beer.

CAROL Get him a beer, Kenny.

KENNY Why is it always my turn?

ALFRED Not now, thanks.

CAROL He doesn't drink.

ALFRED I'll drink later.

CAROL You don't drink. You don't fight.

PATSY I fight, Daddy!

MARJORIE Carol, leave the poor boy alone.

CAROL (*Shouts*) *How many times do I have to tell you—*

MARJORIE (*Hurt*) I'm sorry. Whatever I do is wrong.

KENNY (*Doing Bogart*) Hey. What's dat? Dat my best goil talking? Hey.
(*He hugs her from behind*)

MARJORIE (*Kittenish*) Kenny! What will Alfred think? He'll think you're always making love to your mother!

CAROL (*Sourly*) He *is* always making love to his mother.

MARJORIE Well, someone has to—(*She smiles into* CAROL'S *glare*) dear.

PATSY (*Serving drinks*) What's this? What's this? I thought I was your best girl, Kenny?
(KENNY *tries to release* MARJORIE *and go to* PATSY. *She grabs his arms and holds on*)

MARJORIE (*To* ALFRED) When Patsy lived at home we used to go on like this all the time.

KENNY (*Whining*) Let go, Mom!

CAROL   Stop all this silliness and drink your liquor!
   (MARJORIE *releases* KENNY, *who goes over to* PATSY)

MARJORIE   (*Flirtatious*)   You're an intelligent-sounding
   man, Alfred. I would think if you spoke to these people
   quietly and sensibly they'd realize the sort of person you
   were and go away.

ALFRED   What can you say that's sensible to a drunk who
   you haven't been staring at, when he shoves you in the
   chest and says, "Who do you think you're staring at,
   fatface?" If you deny you've been staring at him, you've
   as much as called him a liar. For that you get hit. If
   you stutter in confusion, you've as much as admitted
   your guilt. For that you get hit. If you tell him you were
   staring at him because he reminds you of a kid you went
   to school with in Chicago, he turns out to *hate* Chicago.
   And for that you get hit.

MARJORIE   (*To* PATSY)   I didn't know he went to school in
   Chicago. Nobody tells me anything. (*To* ALFRED) We
   went to Chicago in 1946. Whereabout did you live in
   Chicago, Alfred?

ALFRED   The South Side.

MARJORIE   I'm not comfortable eating away from home.
   Well, that's another story. Does your family still live
   there?

27

ALFRED   I don't know.

CAROL   You don't know! What kind of answer is that?
You don't know! That's the silliest answer I've ever
heard!

ALFRED   I haven't kept up contact.
        (CAROL *frowns, disapproving*)

MARJORIE   There seems to be so little cohesiveness in
families today. *We* never went anywhere. We were too
unsophisticated to know that home wouldn't serve. (*At*
PATSY)   Today they run off here, they run off there—

KENNY (*Hugs her*)   I'll never leave you, Mom.

CAROL   Will you two break it up? How about another
round? Name your poison, Alfred.

MARJORIE (*Sadly*)   We've had our share of tragedy—

PATSY (*Warning*)   Mother—
        (*Phone rings.* CAROL *starts for it.* MARJORIE *beats
        him to it*)

MARJORIE   Let me, dear. It's never for you. Hello. (*Amplified sound of heavy breathing*)   Hello. Hello. Who is
this? Hello. (PATSY *starts toward her*)   The most curi-
ous business. Hello.
        (PATSY *takes phone, listens and hangs up*)

PATSY (*To* MARJORIE) You get it too.

CAROL What? (PATSY *looks toward* MARJORIE, *who smiles but does not answer*) What?

MARJORIE Never mind, dear. It's not important.
(CAROL *frustrated*. PATSY *goes to him*)

PATSY The Breather, Daddy. Do you get many of these, Mother?

MARJORIE He's the pleasantest of the lot. You should hear the ones who *talk!* I grit my teeth, turn my ears *right* off, and wait politely for them till they've finished their business.

CAROL (*Exasperated*) Will somebody please explain to me—

PATSY I get them every night. You know, Daddy—these oddballs who call you up at all hours and just *breathe* at you.

CAROL (*Appalled*) Late at night? They breathe at you? (*To* ALFRED) And you don't fight back?!
(*Doorbell*)

MARJORIE I'll get it! (*She crosses to door and opens peephole*) Who is it? I'm sorry, I can't understand you! Will you please stand closer to the peephole? I can't see you—

take your hand off the peephole. I warn you, I'm calling the doorman! (PATSY *starts for door.* MARJORIE *shuts peephole and intercepts her. She returns, musing*) If it happens once, it happens a dozen times a day. And we gave that doorman fifteen dollars for Christmas.

> (PATSY *protectively puts her arms around her.* MAR-JORIE *lightly shrugs it off*)

CAROL (*To* ALFRED) *What are you going to do if you're on the street with my daughter?*

PATSY Don't be silly, Daddy. I'm quite capable of taking care of myself.

KENNY (*Proudly*) She's as strong as an ox. When we were kids we used to wrestle all the time. I always lost.

PATSY (*Enjoying herself*) Daddy, I assure you, no one's going to pick on me. I'm a big, strapping girl! I don't daydream, and I *do* hit back. When I take Alfred home every night, I guarantee you there's no trouble.

CAROL You let *her* take you home?

PATSY He doesn't *let* me. He doesn't have anything to say about it. Every time I leave him alone somebody in this crazy city mugs him. Once I have him safely married (CAROL *and* KENNY *wince*), I won't let him out of my

sight for five minutes. (*Pinches* ALFRED) He's too cute to get beat up—by anyone but me.
> (*She throws a playful but entirely masculine punch at* ALFRED. *He smiles happily as it connects.* KENNY *exits. Offstage door slam*)

MARJORIE Aren't they adorable?

CAROL (*Quietly to* MARJORIE) What did I tell you about him, huh? Didn't I predict?

MARJORIE I think he's very sweet.

CAROL That's a sure sign. You think they're *all* sweet. I'll be damned (*Louder*) if I'd let myself stand by and let a woman fight my battles for me.

PATSY (*Hugging* CAROL *from behind*) They don't make frontier fighters like my father any more.

MARJORIE (*Looks about*) Kenny! (*Shakes her head in exasperation and smiles seductively at* ALFRED) Alfred, would you mind giving me a hand?
> (*They exit*)

CAROL (*Delighted*) Come on. Stop being silly. Cut it out.

PATSY (*Playful, squeezing tighter*) Let's see how good you are, tiger. Break my grip! Come on!
> (*Momentary look of panic in* CAROL's *eyes.* PATSY *releases him. They laugh*)

31

CAROL (*Slaps her cheek playfully*) Who's my baby girl, eh? (*Suddenly serious*) I wish you had as much brains as you have brawn.

PATSY You don't like him, do you, Daddy?

CAROL Don't put words in my mouth.

PATSY Then you *do* like him?

CAROL I want to know more about him before I make up my mind—

PATSY Not to like him.

CAROL Don't bully me, young lady. You know I don't like it when you bully me.

PATSY You *love* it when I bully you.

CAROL (*Chuckles*) You're too damned fast for the old man. (*Slaps her cheek playfully*) But I know a thing or two. (*Deadly serious*) Never settle for less.

PATSY Daddy, I'm *not*!

CAROL Never sell yourself short.

PATSY Oh, Daddy, when have I *ever*—

CAROL   The right man will come along.

PATSY   Daddy, I'm twenty-seven. The right men all got married two years ago. They won't get their first divorce for another five years, and I just don't have the time, the inclination, or the kind of looks that can afford to wait.

CAROL   I don't want to hear you knocking yourself. You've got ten people working under you! (*Proudly*) You're five-foot eight!

PATSY   After a while it doesn't *matter* that you can do everything better than everyone else. I've been the best for years now, and all it comes down to is that I'm efficient.

CAROL   You don't know what you're talking about. You're very popular.

PATSY   When they want a woman they can collapse without shame in front of—they come to me.

CAROL   Why not? You're trusted!

PATSY   Oh, to meet a man who *is* ashamed to collapse in front of me! Daddy, I get dizzy spells from being so strong; I get migraine from being so damnably depend-able. I'm tired of being Mother Earth! Daddy, Alfred's the *only* man I know who isn't waiting for me to save

him. Don't you know how that makes me feel? God
help me, I've got to save him!
(*She embraces* CAROL, *who blissfully returns embrace.* ALFRED *enters uncorking the wine and sur-
veys scene.* CAROL *quickly disengages*)

MARJORIE (*Enters wheeling serving cart*) Come an' git
it! (*To* ALFRED *as she starts serving*) My mother always
used to say that to us children at mealtimes. I've always
found it a charming family tradition. So I say, "Come an'
git it!" to our children. I dream of the day when I can
hear Patsy say, "Come an' git it!" to her children. (*To*
KENNY, *who is offstage*) Kenny! Didn't you hear me say
come an' git it, or do you need a special invitation?

KENNY (*Still offstage*) In a minute!

MARJORIE Not a minute, young man! Right now! (*To*
ALFRED) It's so stuffy in here. Alfred, would you open a
window like a good fellow? (*Sounds of toilet flush, offstage door slam.* CAROL *rises*) No, I asked Alfred, dear.
(KENNY *enters with paperback, passes* CAROL, *who
outpaces* ALFRED *to window*)

CAROL (*Struggling with window*) It's all right. It's perfectly all right. (*Gives up*) Son of a bitch! (*To* ALFRED)
The son of a bitch refuses to open!
(ALFRED *gives strong jerk. Window opens. Traffic,
construction and airplane noise*)

MARJORIE Thank you, Alfred (*To* CAROL) You see, I had my reasons.
 (*Light film of soot wafts through window*)

CAROL I loosened it!

KENNY He loosened it! That's a riot!
 (*Convulses himself*)

CAROL (*Slams window shut. To* KENNY) Now *you* open it! (KENNY *airily dismisses him*) No, you're the smart one around here! Let's see you open it!

MARJORIE I spent the whole day cooking. Can't we eat now and open and close windows later?

CAROL It won't take a second. Well, young man, are you going to try or are you just going to sit back and laugh at the earnest efforts of your betters? (KENNY, *with arrogant mockery, rises, tries and fails to open window. He shrugs, smiles, and ambles back to table.* ALFRED *and* CAROL *follow. All sit*) You're not so smart now, are you?

MARJORIE Will someone please open the window? (PATSY *leaps up before* ALFRED *can rise, strides to window, kicks off heels, jerks window open. Noise and dust.* KENNY *and* CAROL *bend over their plates, embarrassed.* PATSY *returns to table*) When Patsy lived at home I always knew I had someone to do my heavy lifting for me.

35

I was always too petite. (PATSY *shrinks over her plate.
All quietly eat*) You don't know what a pleasure it is
to have my family all together this way. (*Lights flicker
and black out, as before. Sounds of eating*) Do you know
that in the *big* power failure some people stood in the
subways, in total darkness, for as long as four hours
without bringing their newspapers down from in front
of their faces? (*Long silence. Eating sounds.* MARJORIE
lights candles) It would be nice if someone else, on
occasion, would think of lighting the candles. Kenny,
come back here! (*Offstage door slam.* KENNY *returns
carrying paperback*) I'm the watchdog around here,
Alfred. I can imagine what Patsy must have told you
about me.

PATSY (*Bored*)   Must you, Mother?
        (*They exchange long stares.* MARJORIE *rises and
        exits. Door slam. Lights go on*)

CAROL (*Up quickly*)   I'm going to make myself another
drink.

KENNY   Make me one.

PATSY   Me too.

ALFRED   Scotch neat.
        (CAROL *stops, stares at him, goes over to bar, grin-
        ning. Offstage sounds of toilet flush, door slam*)

MARJORIE (*Enters carrying photographs*) It's gotten a little chilly in here . . . (KENNY *up before anyone can move. He slams down window.* CAROL *serves drinks.* MARJORIE *frowns as* PATSY *accepts drink*) That's your second tonight, isn't it? And I suppose you're still smoking as much? (PATSY *salutes with glass. Drains it*) Drinks like a fish. Smokes like a chimney. (PATSY *has mock cough spasm*) It's the ones who think they're indestructible who do the most damage to themselves. Kenny, is that a new drink? (KENNY *bolts drink.* MARJORIE *shakes head, looks warily at* CAROL. *He bolts drink, scratches his hand nervously. To* ALFRED, *with photographs*) You're a photographer, Alfred, so I thought you'd be interested in seeing these pictures of Patsy's dead brother, Steve.

(PATSY *covers her face with her hands*)

ALFRED   He looks very handsome in his swimsuit.

MARJORIE   He won five gold cups. He was ten years older than Patsy.

KENNY   Fifteen years older than me.

ALFRED   He looks very handsome in his baseball uniform.

MARJORIE   He only pitched no-hitters.

ALFRED (*Handing back pictures*)   Thank you for letting me see them.

MARJORIE This one was taken after he came home from the war, a hero.

ALFRED He looks very handsome in his uniform. What do these double bars signify?

MARJORIE He was a captain. A hero. He bombed Tokyo. When his country called on him to serve again he bombed Korea. A brilliant future in electronics, not an enemy in the world, whoever dreamed he'd be shot down in his tracks on the corner of Ninety-seventh Street and Amsterdam Avenue. (*Gathers up pictures*) But I won't bore you with our tragedy.

PATSY (*Explodes*) Damn it, Mother! Must I go through this every time I bring a man home to dinner? (MARJORIE *sobs, rushes off. Door slam*) Patsy's done it again!

KENNY (*Admiring*) Boy, I'd be killed if I ever talked like that.

CAROL I don't approve of your behavior, young lady. Your mother worked long and hard and imaginatively over this dinner. (PATSY *puts a cigarette in her mouth*) And she's right about your smoking too much, Goddamnit!
    (PATSY *turns to* CAROL, *cigarette in mouth, waiting for a light. He resists for a moment, then lights it*)

PATSY (*In command*) Thank you. (CAROL *scratches his hand. Softly to* ALFRED) I'm sorry you had to be subjected to this, honey. (*To* CAROL, *taking his hand, placating*) Alfred knows all about Steve, Daddy.

(CAROL *revives*)

ALFRED   They still don't have any idea who did it?

CAROL   That's all right. The boys down at Homicide have worked long and hard and imaginatively on this case. (*With pride*) Many have become close personal friends. (*Toilet flush, door slam.* MARJORIE *enters, eyes red but smiling. She is clutching a handkerchief.* KENNY *rises and exits in her direction. Door slam*)

MARJORIE   (*At serving cart*)   We can't disappoint our guest with only one helping.

ALFRED   No, thank you, Mrs. Newquist. I've had plenty.

PATSY (*Ingratiating*)   It was delicious, Mother!

CAROL   It was delicious!

MARJORIE   Kenny! Where are you?

KENNY (*Offstage, muffled*)   It was delicious!

MARJORIE (*To* ALFRED)   A big man like you. Now, don't just stand on politeness—

ALFRED   No. I'm really quite stuffed, thank you.

MARJORIE (*To* PATSY) Well, then I'll have to turn to my best customer.

PATSY I couldn't eat another bite, Mother. It was delicious.

CAROL I couldn't eat another bite. It was delicious.

KENNY (*Offstage, muffled*) *I couldn't eat another bite. It was delicious!* (*Toilet flush. Door slam. He enters carrying paperback*) I could use another drink, though.
>   (*He detours on his way back from bar to surreptitiously pick up* PATSY's *heels in front of window. Takes them to his seat*)

CAROL (*Rises*) I think I'll have another. (*At the bar*) Patsy?

PATSY (*Rises*) Leave out the water this time.
>   (*She goes to bar*)

ALFRED Scotch neat.

MARJORIE (*Not really approving*) Well, it's a special occasion.

PATSY (*Looks around*) Where the devil did I leave my shoes?
>   (KENNY *looks away*)

MARJORIE (*Gathering photographs from table*) I'd better put these in a safe place before someone spills liquor on them. I'm sorry to have taken your time, Alfred. Knowing you were a photographer I thought you'd be interested. (*Waits for response; there is none*) Exactly what sort of work do you do? Portraits?

ALFRED No.

PATSY (*Returns protectively. Hands* ALFRED *drink*) Stop cross-examining him, Mother.

MARJORIE I don't know why everything I do is wrong. Alfred, do you object to my asking you about your work?

ALFRED It's not all that interesting, actually.

MARJORIE You don't do portraits?

ALFRED No.

MARJORIE Do you do magazine photography?

ALFRED No.

PATSY Has somebody got a cigarette?

MARJORIE (*To* PATSY) Must you? Can't you give in to me just this once? (CAROL *sits, hands* PATSY *cigarette.* KENNY *lights it. Barely in control, to* ALFRED) Advertising photography?

ALFRED Well, I used to. I don't any more.

CAROL   Fashion photography?
(*He nudges* KENNY)

KENNY (*Rolls his eyes*)   Woo! Woo!
(CAROL *and* KENNY *exchange joyful glances. Stifle laughs*)

ALFRED   It's sort of complicated. Are you sure you want to hear?

PATSY (*Resigned*)   You may as well—

ALFRED   Well, I began as a commercial photographer—

PATSY   He began as a painter.

ALFRED   A very bad painter.

PATSY   Says you!

CAROL   *For Christ sakes, will you let the boy finish!*
(*All, including* CAROL, *are surprised by outburst*)

ALFRED   I began as a commercial photographer, and was doing sort of well at it.

PATSY   *Sort of* well! You should see his portfolio. He's had work in *Holiday, Esquire, The New Yorker, Vogue*—

CAROL   *Vogue!*

KENNY (*Rolls his eyes*) Woo! Woo!
(*He and* CAROL *exchange nudges, joyful glances.*
PATSY *glares. They subside*)

ALFRED It's an overrated business. But after a couple of
years of doing sort of well (PATSY *slaps his hand lightly*)
at it, things began to go wrong. I began losing my people.
Somehow I got my heads chopped off. Or out of focus.
Or *terrible* expressions on my models. I'd have them ex-
amining a client's product like this (*Expression of dis-
taste*)—the agencies began to wonder if I didn't have
some editorial motive in mind. Well, it wasn't true. But
once they'd *planted* the idea—I couldn't help thinking
of plane crashes every time I shot an airline ad, or deaths
on the highway every time I shot an automobile ad, or
price-rigging every time I shot a pharmaceutical ad—
and power failures when I shot Con Edison ads.
(*Lights go out*)

MARJORIE I don't mean to interrupt, dear. (*Lights match
and candles*) "How far better it is to light a match than
curse the darkness." My mother told us that. Go on.

ALFRED Well, my career suffered. But there was nothing
I could do about it. The harder I tried to straighten out,
the fuzzier my people got and the clearer my objects. Soon
my people disappeared entirely, they just somehow never
came out. But the objects I was shooting—brilliantly clear.
(*Snaps fingers. Lights come back on*) So I began to do
a lot of catalogue work. (MARJORIE *blows out candles*)

43

Pictures of medical instruments, things like that. There was—well, the best way to describe it is—a *seductiveness* I was able to draw out of inanimate things that other photographers didn't seem to be able to get. I suppose the real break came with the I.B.M. show. They had me shoot thirty of their new models. They hired a gallery and had a computer show. One hundred and twenty color pictures of computers. It got some very strange (*Whimsical smile*) notices, the upshot of which was that the advertising business went "thing" crazy, and I became commercial again.

MARJORIE   You must be extremely talented.

ALFRED (*More to himself than to family*)   I got *sick* of it! Where the hell are standards? That's what I kept asking myself. Those people will take anything! Hell, if I gave them a picture of *shit* they'd give me an award for it! (*All stiffen.* PATSY *looks wary*)

MARJORIE   Language, young man!

ALFRED   Mm? So that's what I do now.

CAROL (*Hesitantly*)   What?

ALFRED   Take pictures of shit.

MARJORIE   Language! Language! This is *my* table!

ALFRED I don't mean to offend you, Mrs. Newquist. I've been shooting shit for a year now, and I've already won a half-dozen awards.

MARJORIE (*Slowly thaws*) Awards?

ALFRED And *Harper's Bazaar* wants me to do its spring issue.

KENNY (*Rolling his eyes*) Woo! Woo!

CAROL (*Angry, to* KENNY) *Don't kid!*

MARJORIE That's a very respectable publication. (*Rises shakily, gathers up dishes*) It all sounds very impressive. (*She exits with serving cart*)

CAROL (*Up quickly, about to speak, when phone rings. He goes for it, all the while glaring at* ALFRED) Hello. (*Amplified breathing*) Look, I don't know who you are, but you're not dealing with helpless women now! *You people!* You young people today! Destroy! Destroy! When are you going to find time to build? In my day we couldn't afford telephones to breathe in! You ought to get down on your hands and knees and be grateful! Why isn't anybody GRATEFUL—(PATSY *takes receiver away, hangs up*) Excuse me.
    (*He exits*)

PATSY Kenny, would you mind—

KENNY (*Grins*) It's my house.

PATSY (*Threatening*) Kenny! (PATSY *starts for him. He jumps up from table, grabbing his drink, and runs out. He has on* PATSY's *heels. Door slams. Offstage sound of distant sirens*) Well, my friend—

ALFRED They asked me what I did for a living.
(*Shrugs*)

PATSY (*Gives him a long stare*) I don't know what to do with you. You're the toughest reclamation job *I've* ever had.

ALFRED You might try retiring on your laurels. You've reformed five fags in a row, why press your luck with a nihilist?

PATSY *Because you're wrong!* (*Calms herself*) Alfred, *every* age has problems. And people somehow manage . . . *to be happy*! I'm sorry, I don't mean to bully you . . . Yes, I do mean to bully you. Alfred, do you know how I wake up every morning of my life? With a smile on my face! And for the rest of the day I come up against an unending series of challenges to wipe that smile off my face. The Breather calls . . . ex-boy friends call to tell me they're getting married . . . someone tries to break into the apartment while I'm dressing . . . there's a drunk asleep in the elevator . . . three minutes after I'm out on the street my camel coat turns brown . . . the subway stalls . . . the man standing next to me presses his body against mine . . . the up elevator jams . . . rumors start buzzing around the office that we're about to be automated . . . the down elevator jams . . . all the taxis are off-duty . . . the air on Lexington Avenue is purple . . . a man tries to pick me up on the bus . . . another man follows me home . . . I step in the door and the Breather's on the phone . . . isn't that enough to wipe the smile off anybody's face? Well, it doesn't wipe it off *mine!* Because for every bad thing there are two good things—no—*four* good things! There are friends . . . and a wonderful job . . . and tennis . . . and skiing . . . and traveling . . . and musicals . . . and driving in the country . . . and flying your own airplane . . . and staying up all night to see the sun rise. (ALFRED *goes into his daydream*) Alfred, come back here! (*Long pause*) Alfred, if everything is so hopeless—why do anything?

ALFRED   Okay.

PATSY   That's why you don't hit back.

ALFRED   There isn't much point, is there?

PATSY   (*Explodes*) *Do you know what you're talking about? Do you have the slightest idea* (*Catches herself, shakes her head*)—I always talk like my father when I'm in this house. Alfred . . . if you feel that way about things . . . why get *married?*

47

ALFRED   You said you wanted to.

PATSY   (*Turns away*)   I find this a very unpleasant conversation.

ALFRED   (*Dryly*)   Patsy, let's not turn this into a "critical
conversation," just because you're not getting your way.
I'm for getting married.

PATSY   (*Dryly*)   Thanks.

ALFRED   (*After a long, tense pause*)   So it is a "critical
conversation."
       (*He starts off*)

PATSY   Where do you think you're going? (*He exits*)
Alfred! (*Starts after him, muttering to herself*) He
doesn't know how to fight; *that's* why I'm not winning.
(*Exits and brings him back*) Damn it! Aren't you willing
to battle over *anything*? Even *me*?
       (*She anticipates what he is about to say*)

ALFRED *and* PATSY   There isn't much point, is there?
       (*She bear-hugs him*)

PATSY   At least say you love me.

ALFRED *and* PATSY   I'm not sure I know what love is.

PATSY (*Slaps him in the stomach*)   Okay. The gauntlet's
flung! You've had it, buster! I'm going to marry you,

48

make you give me a house, entrap you into a half-dozen children, and seduce you into a life so remorselessly satisfying that within two years under my management you'll come to me with a camera full of baby pictures and say: "Life can be beautiful!"

ALFRED   And ugly. More often ugly.

PATSY   You'll give me a piano to sing around. And a fireplace to lie in front of. And each and every Christmas we will send out *personalized* Christmas cards—with a group family portrait on the front—taken by *Alfred Chamberlain*. Daddy! Mother! I have an announcement! (CAROL *and* MARJORIE *rush in. Sounds of toilet flush, door slam.* KENNY *rushes in, adjusting his trousers*) Alfred and I are getting married! (CAROL *and* KENNY *freeze*) Next week!
     (CAROL *sits down heavily*)

MARJORIE   (*Beaming*)   I've always dreamed of a wedding in my living room! Oh, there's so much to do. (*Kisses them*) You've got yourself a fine young man. And so accomplished! We'll have to let Dr. Paterson know right away—

ALFRED   (*To* PATSY)   Who?

PATSY   The minister, dopey.

ALFRED   (*To* MARJORIE, *picking up phone*)   Mrs. Newquist—(*Sound of amplified breathing.* MARJORIE *quickly hangs up. Picks up again and begins to dial*) Mrs. New-quist, when you speak to the minister, you'd better tell him—we don't want any mention of God in the ceremony.

CAROL I'm going to have him arrested.
       (*All freeze, stare at* ALFRED. *Blackout. Street noises, sirens, etc.*)

The Newquist apartment, one month later. ALFRED, PATSY, CAROL *and* MARJORIE *sit quietly.* CAROL *looks at his watch, rises, begins to pace.* PATSY *places a calming hand on* ALFRED's *arm.* MARJORIE, *the only one unperturbed, smiles gamely. Doorbell.* CAROL *crosses to door.*

MARJORIE   Ask who it is first!
        (CAROL *opens door. The* JUDGE *enters, a portly, well-dressed man of about* CAROL's *age*)

CAROL (*Softly, as if at a wake*)   Jerry. You don't know how I appreciate this.
        (*The* JUDGE *nods, accepts* CAROL's *handshake, looks at his watch*)

JUDGE (*Softly*)   Nice to see you again, Mrs. Newquist. Are these the youngsters? (CAROL *nods*) No God in the ceremony. Does she live away from home? (CAROL *nods*) It begins there.

MARJORIE (*Softly*)   You'll have to pardon the mess, Judge Stern.

JUDGE   You have a second girl, don't you, Carol?

CAROL A boy.

JUDGE A son!

CAROL A boy.

MARJORIE (*To* PATSY *and* ALFRED) Children, this is—

CAROL I'll do it! Judge Jerome M. Stern, one of my oldest and dearest—

JUDGE I don't have much time. If the grownups will please excuse us—
(*Looks to* CAROL *and* MARJORIE, *who reluctantly start to exit as* KENNY *enters*)

MARJORIE Out, young man!

KENNY Why can't I ever—
(MARJORIE *shoves him. They exit together*)

JUDGE (*Stares at* ALFRED *and* PATSY *for a long moment*) Sit down please. (*They remain standing*) I can't talk unless I'm the tallest. (PATSY *sits, and eases* ALFRED *down beside her*) No God in the ceremony, mm? Getting a lot of turn-downs, aren't you? Surprising, isn't it, how the name of God is still respected in this town. (*Studies* PATSY) Carol Newquist's daughter. (*Sighs*) Your father and me go back a long ways, young lady. He's done me a lot of favors. Got me tickets to shows—(*Sighs. Shakes*

his head) I'd *like* to help him out (*Shakes his head*)—
My mother, thank God she's not alive today, landed in
this country sixty-five years ago. Four infants in her
arms. Kissed the sidewalk the minute she got off the
boat, she was so happy to be out of Russia alive. Across
the ocean alive. More dead than alive, if you want to
know the truth. Sixteen days in the steerage. Fifteen
people got consumption. Five died. My father, thank
God he's not alive today, came over two years earlier,
sixty-seven years ago. Worked like a son of a bitch to
earn our passage (*To* PATSY)—Pardon my French. You
don't want God in the ceremony, so you're probably
familiar with it. My father worked fourteen hours a day
in a sweatshop on lower Broadway. Number three-fifteen.
Our first apartment was a five-flight walk-up, four-and-a-
half-room cold-water flat. With the bathtub in the
kitchen and the toilet down the hall. One-forty-two
Hester Street. Three families used the toilet. An Italian
family. A colored family. A Jewish family. Three families with different faiths, but one thing each of those
families had in common. They had in common the sac-
rifices each of them had to make to get where they were.
What they had in common was *persecution*. So they
weren't so *glib* about God. God was in my mother's every
conversation about how she got her family out of
Russia, thank God, in one piece. About the pogroms.
The steerage. About those who *didn't* make it. Got sick
and died. Who could they ask for help? If not God, then
*who? The Great Society? The Department of Welfare?
Travelers Aid?* Mind you, I'm a good Democrat, I'm not

knocking these things. Although sometimes—there weren't any handouts in those days. This city was a—a—*concrete jungle* to the families that came here. They had to carve homes and lives out of *concrete*—cold *concrete!* You think they didn't call on God, these poor suffering greenhorns? You see the suit I'm wearing? Expensive? Custom-made? My father, thank God he's not alive today, worked sixteen hours a day in a shop on Broome Street, and his artistry for a tenth of what you pay today makes meat loaf out of this suit. One-forty-five dash one-forty-seven Broome Street. So tired, so broken in spirit, when he climbed the six flights of stairs each night to the three-room unheated cold-water flat the five of us were crowded in—one-seventy-one Attorney Street—that he did not have the strength to eat. *The man did not have the strength to eat.* Turning thinner and yellower by the day for lack of *what?* A well-balanced diet? Too much cholesterol? Too many carbohydrates and starchy substances in his blood? Not on your sweet life! For lack of *everything!* What was God to my father? I'll tell you—sit down, I'm not finished!—I'll tell you what God was to my father! God got my father up those six and a half flights of stairs, not counting the stoop, every night. God got my mother, worn gray from lying to her children about a better tomorrow she didn't believe in, up each morning with enough of the failing strength that finally deserted her last year in Miami Beach at the age of ninety-one, to face another day of hopelessness and despair. Thirty-one-thirty-five Biscayne Boulevard. God. Do you know how old I was when I first had to go out and work? Look at these hands? The hands of a professional man? Not on your sweet life! The hands of a *worker*! I *worked*! These hands toiled from the time I was nine— strike that, *seven*. Every morning up at five, dressing in the pitch black to run down seven flights of stairs, thirteen steps to a flight—I'll never forget them—to run five blocks to the Washington market, unpacking crates for seventy-five cents a week. A dollar if I worked Sundays. Maybe! Based on the goodness of the bosses' hearts. Where was my God then? Where, on those bitter cold mornings, with my hands so blue with frostbite they looked like ladies' gloves, was God? Here! In my heart! Where He was, has been, will always be! Till the day they carry me feet first out of these chambers—knock wood, God grant it's soon. My first murder trial—where are you going? I'm not finished!

ALFRED (*At the door*) You're not going to marry us.

JUDGE I'm not finished! Don't be a smart punk! (ALFRED *exits*) You're a know-it-all wise guy smart punk, aren't you? I've seen your kind! *You'll come up before me again!* (PATSY *exits*. CAROL *and* MARJORIE *enter. The* JUDGE *looks at his watch. Very coldly, after a long pause*) He made me very late.

Blackout

The lights come up. The Newquist apartment is decorated for a wedding. The guests are gathered around the wedding cake, having their picture taken. Ad lib laughter on the camera flash. Two gunshots are heard coming from the window. The guests rush to the window.

FIRST GUEST   Where is it—

SECOND GUEST   Up there!

THIRD GUEST   Where?

FOURTH GUEST   There!

SECOND GUEST   He's got a rifle!

FIFTH GUEST   Somebody call the police!

SECOND GUEST   He's only a kid!

THIRD GUEST   Kids can kill.

FOURTH GUEST   I think somebody should call the police!

FIFTH GUEST   I think Carol should call the police.

SIXTH GUEST   An old lady got murdered in my building in front of thirty witnesses.

THIRD GUEST   And everybody just stood there, right?

FIRST GUEST   Call the police.
   (*Guests have begun to drift away from the window. Two more gunshots, which they ignore*)

THIRD GUEST   I learned to kill with the edge of a rolled-up newspaper.

FIRST GUEST   I carry a hunting knife.
   (*The family enters and the guests applaud*)

CAROL (*To* FIRST GUEST)   Nothing like a little excitement—
   (*Loses smile as he watches* PATSY *cross to* ALFRED *and hug him. Scattered cheers, drinks raised in toast*)

MARJORIE (*To* SECOND GUEST)   Aren't they an attractive couple? He's so big. It's wonderful to marry a big man. There are so many complications when you marry a man shorter than yourself.

CAROL (*To* THIRD GUEST)   I gave them twenty-five hundred. It's just a token.

57

MARJORIE (*To* SECOND GUEST) And she's so big herself. Many's the time I gave up hope she'd find a man bigger than she is.

CAROL (*To* FOURTH GUEST) Twenty-five hundred—

MARJORIE (*To* SECOND GUEST) Or heavier. It's always amazed me the size of her. I've always been such a little peanut.

ALFRED (*To* FIFTH GUEST) No. My family's not here.

MARJORIE (*To* SECOND GUEST) You'd think almost anybody I'd married would have to be bigger than me; well, that's the way life works out.

KENNY (*To* SIXTH GUEST) I haven't made up my mind. I may go into teaching.

MARJORIE (*To* THIRD GUEST) He's a world-famous photographer, you know. He does collages for *Harper's Bazaar*. (*General laughter.* MARJORIE *looks around to see what she's missing*) And he's terribly independent. I always thought Patsy was independent, but this time I think she's met her match.

PATSY (*To* SECOND GUEST) Well, the first year at least we'll live at my place.

MARJORIE (*To* THIRD GUEST)   No God in the ceremony, he says. Yes, God in the ceremony, she says. Well, you see who won that one.

CAROL   Twenty-five hundred—

ALFRED (*To* FIRST GUEST)   No. My family isn't here.

MARJORIE (*To* THIRD GUEST)   I would never have the nerve to stand up to her. Her father has never stood up to her. Her brother has never stood up to her. But this time she didn't get her way. (*Gaily*) There's not going to be any God in the ceremony.

KENNY (*To* SECOND GUEST)   What I really want to do is direct films.

MARJORIE (*To* FOURTH GUEST)   Poor children, these past few weeks they've really had a rough time of it. Nobody wanted to marry them. Even the state of New York has God in the ceremony. They looked everywhere.

ALFRED (*To* SECOND GUEST)   No. My family's not here.

MARJORIE (*To* FOURTH GUEST)   Ethical Culture told them they didn't have to have God in the ceremony, but they had to have ethical culture in the ceremony.

PATSY (*To* FIRST GUEST) I plan to go on working into my eighth month.

MARJORIE (*To* FOURTH GUEST) Finally, they found this man (*Doorbell. All pause tensely.* CAROL *checks peephole, unlocks door.* DUPAS *enters*)—there he is now—Alfred found him, really—Reverend Dupas. (*Pronounced Doo-pah*)

ALFRED (*Escorting* PATSY *over to* DUPAS) Henry. (*Mimed greetings and handshakes*)

MARJORIE (*To* FOURTH GUEST) He doesn't have much of a handshake, but Alfred says he's very well established in Greenwich Village. He's pastor of the First Existential Church—the one that has that sign in front that says—

DUPAS (*To* ALFRED) My bike wouldn't start up.

MARJORIE (*To* FOURTH GUEST, *quoting*) "Christ died for our sins. Dare we make his martyrdom meaningless by not committing them?"

CAROL (*To* DUPAS, *with feigned good cheer*) No atheists in foxholes these days, eh, Reverend? They've all gone into the ministry.

MARJORIE (*To* FOURTH GUEST) Two Sundays ago he gave a sermon on the moral affirmation in Alfred's photographs.

CAROL   Can I see you for a minute in private, Reverend?
(*He leads him off*)

KENNY (*Starts off*)   Hey, that's *my* room!

PATSY (*Looking after them, puzzled*)   They'll be right out.

MARJORIE   They'll be right out, dear.

KENNY   How do they know I don't have to go in there?
(*Starts off.* MARJORIE *blocks his way*) I need a *hand-kerchief!* (*Tries to get around her but is blocked*) I've
got a right to go into my own room!

MARJORIE (*Conciliatory*)   Why don't you go into the
bathroom, dear?

KENNY (*To* PATSY)   Why can't you do your things in
your own room?

PATSY   Kenny—(*Reaches for him. He turns away*) Why
are you mad at me?
        (KENNY *storms away. The phone rings.* KENNY *gets
        it. Amplified breathing*)

KENNY (*Into phone*)   Faggot!
        (*Hangs up. Sound of gunshots. All ignore them.*
        CAROL *enters with his arm around* DUPAS, *who dis-
        engages and crosses to* ALFRED)

DUPAS (*To* ALFRED) Your father-in-law wants me to sneak the deity into the ceremony.

ALFRED What did you tell him?

DUPAS He offered me a lot of money. I told him I'd make my decision in a few minutes. (DUPAS *checks* CAROL's *whereabouts. He is across room being congratulated, scratching his hand and staring intently at* DUPAS) If it's all right with you I'd like to take the money, and then *not* mention the deity. First Existential can use the money.

ALFRED He'll stop the check.

DUPAS I thought he might. Still, it would serve as a lesson . . .

ALFRED I don't know what to tell you, Henry.

DUPAS Well, we'll see.
(*He crosses over to* CAROL. *They exit*)

KENNY (*Starts off*) I need something out of my bedroom.

MARJORIE Kenny! (*Blocks his way.* KENNY *tries to charge past her. She intercepts and they begin to struggle. With forced gaiety*) Ha! Ha! Look, everybody! We're dancing!
(CAROL *and* DUPAS *enter—wrestling match breaks up.* CAROL, *hiding triumph, crosses over to* ALFRED)

CAROL (*Slaps him on back*) Nervous, young fellow? (ALFRED *turns to look for* PATSY. CAROL *takes him by the arm*) I've been looking forward to this day for a long, long time. It would only take one thing more to make it perfect. (ALFRED *smiles politely, looks for* PATSY. CAROL *squeezes his arm*) To hear you call me Dad.

ALFRED   I didn't call my own father Dad.

CAROL   What did you call him?

ALFRED   I didn't call him anything. The occasion never came up. (*Amiably*) I could call you Carol.

CAROL (*Winces*) Look, if it's this God business that's bothering you, I'm willing to be open-minded. I wouldn't let this on to Marjorie or the kids—(*Winks*) I don't believe in God. But to me it's not a matter of belief in God. It's a matter of belief in institutions. I have great belief in institutions. You couldn't concede me *one* Dad? (*No response*) Not all the time—but every once in a while, "Hello, Dad," "How are you, Dad?"

DUPAS   May we proceed?

CAROL   "You like some of my tobacco, Dad?" (ALFRED *tries to free his arm.* CAROL *hangs on, hisses*) I want an answer! (PATSY *crosses, kisses* CAROL, *takes* ALFRED *away. All take their positions for the ceremony*)

DUPAS (*In a gentle, folksy manner*) You all know why we're here. There is often so much sham about this business of marriage. Everyone accepts it. Ritual. That's why I was so heartened when Alfred asked me to perform this ceremony. He has certain beliefs that I assume you all know. He is an atheist, which is perfectly all right. Really it is. I happen not to be, but inasmuch as this ceremony connotates an abandonment of ritual in the search for truth, I agreed to perform it. First, let me state frankly to you, Alfred, and to you, Patricia, that of the two hundred marriages I have performed, all but seven have failed. So the odds are not good. We don't like to admit it, especially at the wedding ceremony, but it's in the back of all our minds, isn't it? How long will it last? We all think that, don't we? We don't like to bring it out in the open, but we all think that. Well, I say why *not* bring it out in the open? *Why* does one decide to marry? Social pressure? Boredom? Loneliness? Sexual appeasement? Um, Love? I do not put any of these reasons down. Each, in its own way, is adequate. Each is all right. I married a musician last year who wanted to get married in order to stop masturbating. (*Guests stir*) Please don't be startled. I am not putting it down. That marriage did not work. But the man tried. Now the man is separated, and still masturbating—but he is at peace with himself. He tried society's way. So you see, it was not a mistake, it turned out all right. Last month I married a novelist to a painter, with everyone at the wedding under the influence of hallucinogenic drugs. The drug quickened our mental responses but slowed our physical responses. It took two days to perform the ceremony. But never had the words so much meaning. *That* marriage should last. Still, if it does not—well, that will be all right. For, don't you see, *any* step that one takes is useful, is positive, *has* to be positive, because it is part of life. And negation of the previously taken step is positive. It too is part of life. And in this light, and *only* in this light, should marriage be regarded. As a small, single step. If it works—fine! If it fails—fine! Look elsewhere for satisfaction. Perhaps to more marriages—fine! As many as one likes—fine! To homosexuality—fine! To drug addiction—I won't put it down. Each of these is an *answer*—for *somebody*. For Alfred, today's answer is Patsy. For Patsy, today's answer is Alfred. I won't put them down for that. So what I implore you both, Alfred and Patricia, to dwell on as I ask the questions required by the State of New York in order to legally bind you—sinister phrase, that—is that not only are the *legal* questions I ask you meaningless but so, too, are those *inner* questions you ask of yourselves meaningless. Failing one's partner does *not* matter. Sexual disappointment does *not* matter. Nothing can hurt if we do not see it as hurtful. Nothing can destroy if we will not see it as destructive. It is all part of life. Part of what we are. So now, Alfred. Do you take Patricia as your lawfully wedded wife, to love—whatever *that* means—to honor—but is not dishonor, in a sense, a *form* of honor?—to keep her in sickness, in health, in prosperity and adversity—what nonsense!— Forsaking all others—what a shocking invasion of privacy! Rephrase that to more sensibly say: if you *choose* to have affairs you won't feel guilty about them—as long as you both shall live—or as long as you're not bored with each other?

ALFRED (*Numb*) I do.

DUPAS So. Patricia. Do you take Alfred here as your lawfully wedded husband, to love—that harmful word—can't we more wisely say: communicate?—to honor—meaning, I suppose, you won't cut his balls off. Yet some men like that. And to obey—well, my very first look at you told me you were not the type to obey, so I went through the thesaurus and came up with these alternatives: to be loyal, to show fealty, to show devotion, to answer the helm—general enough, I would think, and still leave plenty of room to dominate, in sickness, in health, and all the rest of that gobbledegook, as long as you both shall live?

PATSY (*Struggling to suppress her fury*) I do.

DUPAS Alfred and Patsy. I know now that whatever you do will be all right. And Patsy's father, Carol Newquist —I've never heard that name on a man before, but I'm sure it's all right—I ask you, sir, not to feel guilt over the $250 check you gave me to mention the deity in this ceremony. What you have done is all right. It is part of what you are, what we all are. And I beg you not to be overly perturbed when I do not mention the deity in this ceremony. Betrayal, too, is all right. It is part of what we all are. And Patsy's brother, Kenneth Newquist, in whose bedroom I spent a few moments earlier this afternoon and whose mother proudly told me the decoration was by your hand *entirely*: I beg of you to feel no shame; homosexuality is all right—

> (KENNY *and* CAROL, *followed by* MARJORIE *and* GUESTS, *charge* DUPAS. *Outraged screams and cries as they mob and beat him.* PATSY *staggers off as* DUPAS, *crying "It's all right, it's all right," is driven out the door.* CAROL *turns on* ALFRED *and begins to slug away at his body.* ALFRED, *unflinching, begins to hum*)
>
> *Curtain*

Act Two

Act Two

SCENE I

Four hours later. The Newquist apartment is strewn with wedding litter. ALFRED *and* CAROL *have not moved since last scene. They stand in half dark,* CAROL *sluggishly pounding away at* ALFRED, *who is humming obviously in a dream world. The phone rings several times.* PATSY *enters, answers phone—amplified breathing.*

PATSY (*Into phone*) You're all we need today. (*Hangs up. To* CAROL) Daddy, you've been at it for hours. Will you please come away from there? (*She helps* CAROL *off.* ALFRED *doesn't move. She reenters, stares a long while at him*) Mother's hysterical, Daddy's collapsed and Kenny's disappeared with my wardrobe. I hope you're pleased with your day's work. (*She goes to him*) You can stop daydreaming, Alfred. Nobody's hitting—
      (*Stops. Takes off wedding glove. Cocks back fist. Holds, undecided. Distant gunshot*)

ALFRED (*Coming out of trance*)   I thought it was a very nice ceremony. (*She drops fist*) A little hokey—

PATSY (*Controlling herself*) Alfred? (*Waves hand in front of his face*) What's going to become of us if you go on this way? Weren't you *there*? Weren't you *listen-*

71

ing? I wanted a *wedding!* What in God's name do you use for feelings?

ALFRED   I feel.

PATSY   You don't feel.

ALFRED   Have it your way.

PATSY   There you go again! You won't fight!

ALFRED   You knew I wouldn't fight before you married me. I didn't realize it was a prerequisite.

PATSY   Well, maybe it is. More and more I think it is. If you don't fight you don't feel. If you don't feel you don't love.

ALFRED   I don't know—

PATSY *(Finishing his sentence)*   What love is. Of course you don't know! Because you don't feel.

ALFRED   I feel what I want to feel.

PATSY *(An impulsive kiss)*   It's like kissing white bread. You *don't* feel. Alfred, what is it with you? It gets worse instead of better! I've never had a man do this to me before. It's not just pain you don't feel, you don't feel *pleasure!*

72

ALFRED   I do feel pleasure.

PATSY   About what?

ALFRED   A lot of things.

PATSY   Name one.

ALFRED (*Pause*)   My work.

PATSY   Name another.

ALFRED (*Pause*)   Sleeping.

PATSY   Work and sleeping! That's just great! What about sex?

ALFRED (*Pause*)   It helps you sleep better.

PATSY   Alfred, do you mean half the things you say? You *must* feel something! (*No response. Snaps her fingers in his face. No response. Holds her head*) Jesus Christ! (*Very tired*) Alfred, why did you marry me?

ALFRED (*Pause*)   You're comfortable.

PATSY   *I've never made men comfortable!* I'm popular because I make them *uncertain. You don't understand the first thing about me!*

ALFRED   Patsy, you're screaming.

73

PATSY *Screaming! You son of a bitch, I'll tear you limb from limb! I married you because I wanted to mold you. I loved the man I wanted to mold you into! But you're not even there! How can I mold you if you're not there?*

ALFRED Everything I say makes you unhappy. We used to get along so well—

PATSY Because *I* did all the talking! My God! That's why you were always so quiet! You weren't listening—

ALFRED Sure I was.

PATSY Don't lie, Alfred. I used to stare into those eyes of yours, so warm, so complete with understanding—and now I remember where I've seen those eyes since—When my father was hitting you! *That's* the way you look when you're daydreaming!

ALFRED You don't get hurt that way.

PATSY Honey, I don't want to hurt you. I want to change you. I want to make you see that there is some value in life, that there is some beauty, some tenderness, some things *worth* reacting to. Some things *worth* feeling (*Snaps fingers in front of his eyes*)—Come back here! I swear, Alfred, *nobody* is going to kill you. (*Distant gunshots*) But you've got to take some *chances* some time! What do you want out of life? Just *survival?*

ALFRED (*Nods*) And to take pictures.

PATSY Of shit? It's not enough! It's not, not, not enough! I'm not going to have a surviving marriage, I'm going to have a flourishing marriage! I'm a *woman!* Or, by Jesus, it's about time I became one. I want a *family!* Oh, Christ, Alfred, this is my wedding day. (*Pause. Regains composure*) I want—I want to be married to a big, strong, protective, vital, virile, self-assured man. Who I can protect and take care of. Alfred, honey, you're the first man I've ever gone to bed with where I didn't feel *he* was a lot more likely to get pregnant than I was. (*Desperate*) You owe me something! I've invested everything I believe in you. You've *got* to let me mold you. *Please* let me mold you. (*Regains control*) You've got me begging. You've got me whining, begging and crying. I've never behaved like this in my life. Will you look at this? (*Holds out finger*) That's a tear. I never cried in my life.

ALFRED Me neither.

PATSY You never cried because you were too terrified of everything to let yourself *feel!* You'd have to learn crying from a manual! Chop onions! I never cried because I was too tough—but I felt *everything.* Every slight, every pressure, every vague competition—but I *fought.* And I *won!* There hasn't been a battle since I was five that I haven't won! And the people I fought were happy that I won! Happy! After a while. Alfred, do you have any

75

idea how many people in this town *worship* me? (*To herself, quickly*) Maybe that's the attraction—you don't worship me. Maybe I'd quit loving you if you *did* worship me. Maybe I'd lose all respect for you if you did all the things I want you to do. (*Thinks about it*) Alfred, you've got to change! (*Regains calm*) Listen . . . I'm not saying I'm better or stronger than you are. It's just that we—you and I—have different temperaments. (*Explodes*) *And my temperament is better and stronger than yours!* (*No reaction*) You're a wall! (*Circles around him*) You don't fight! You hardly even listen! Dear God, will somebody please explain to me why I think you're so beautiful? (*Phone rings. She picks it up. Amplified breathing*) *Leave me alone! What do you want out of me? Will you please leave me alone?*

    (ALFRED, *startled by outburst, takes phone away.* PATSY *buries her head in her hands*)

ALFRED (*Into phone*)   She can't talk now.

    (*Hangs up. Distant siren.* PATSY *brings hands down from her face: all life has been drained out of it*)

PATSY (*Empty*)   Alfred, it's all shit. How come I never noticed before?

ALFRED   Patsy—

PATSY (*Empty*)   You were right. I'm just dense. *I'm* the one who doesn't feel. It's all terrible. Terrible. Terrible.

ALFRED   Come on, Patsy.

PATSY (*Empty*) No more reason for *anything*.

ALFRED (*Uncomfortable, weakly*) Mrs. Newquist!

PATSY (*Flat*) The only true feeling is no feeling. The only way to survive. You're one hundred percent right. Hold my hand. (ALFRED *backs away.* PATSY *drops hand*) I'm sorry. I'm not this weak, really. You know how tough I am. I'll be just as tough again, I promise. I just have to learn to be tough about shit. And I will.
    (ALFRED *backs off to a chair*)

ALFRED I feel weak.

PATSY (*Flat*) Alfred, we can't both feel weak at the same time.

ALFRED Patsy, you're beginning to get me nervous. You have to listen to me for a minute—

PATSY (*Flat*) You're right. I'm wrong. Everything is the way you say. (*Begins to withdraw*) You sit. (*Sits*) You get old. (*Freezes*) You die.
    (*Stares as if in one of* ALFRED's *daydreams.* ALFRED *goes to her. Touches her head. No reaction. Lifts her arm. It drops limply to her side. He stares at her horrified, then goes into his daydream stare. He slides into the chair opposite hers. Both stare blankly into space. Phone rings. Many rings.*

77

ALFRED *finally rises, crosses to phone, numbly lifts it. Amplified breathing)*

ALFRED *(Dazed, into phone)* Thanks. I'm up. *(Hangs up. Stares thoughtfully at* PATSY. *Then, slowly, deliberately)* During Korea—I was in school then—the government couldn't decide whether I was a security risk or not—I wore a beard—so they put a mail check on me. *(Passes a hand in front of her eyes. No reaction)* Every day the mail would come later and later. And it would be bent. Corners torn. Never sealed correctly. Like they didn't give a damn whether I knew they were reading my mail or not. I was more of a militant in those days, so I decided to fight fire with fire. I began writing letters to the guy who was reading my mail. I addressed them to myself, of course, but inside they went something like: "Dear Sir: I am not that different from you. All men are brothers. Tomorrow, instead of reading my mail in that dark, dusty hall, why not bring it upstairs where we can check it out together." I never got an answer. So I wrote a second letter. "Dear Sir: There are no heroes, no villains, no good guys, no bad guys. The world is more complicated than that. Come on up where we can open a couple of beers and talk it all out." *(Checks* PATSY. *No reaction)* Again no answer. So then I wrote: "Dear Sir: I've been thinking too much of my own problems, too little of yours. Yours cannot be a happy task—reading another man's mail. It's dull, unimaginative. A job—and let's not mince words—for a hack. Yet, I wonder—can this be the way you see yourself? Do you see yourself as a hack? Do you see yourself as the office slob? Have you ever *wondered* why they stuck *you* with *this* particular job, instead of others who have *less* seniority? Or was it, do you think, that your supervisor looked around the office to see who he'd stick for the job, saw *you* and said, 'No one will miss *him* for a month!'" (*Checks* PATSY) *That* letter never got delivered to me. So *then* I wrote: "Dear Friend: Just a note to advise—you may retain my letters as long as you deem fit. Reread them. Study them. Think them out. Who back at the home office is *out to get you?* Who, at this *very* moment, is sitting at *your* desk, reading *your* mail? I do not say this to be cruel, but because I am the only one left you can *trust*—" No answer. *But,* the next day a man, saying he was from the telephone company, showed up—no complaint had been made—to check the phone. Shaky hands. Bloodshot eyes. A small quaver in the voice. And as he dismembered my phone he said, "Look. What nobody understands is that everybody has his job to do. I got my job. In this case it's repairing telephones. I like it or I don't like it, but it's my job. If I had another job—say, for example, with the F.B.I. or someplace, putting in a wiretap, for example, or reading a guy's mail—*like it or don't like it, it would be my job!* Has anyone got the right to *destroy* a man for doing his job?" I wrote one more letter—expressing my deep satisfaction that he and I had at last made contact, and informing him that the next time he came, say, to read the meter, I had valuable information, photostats, recordings, names and dates, about the conspiracy against him. This letter showed up a week after I mailed it, in a crumpled, grease-stained, and Scotch-taped envelope. The letter itself was torn in half and then clumsily glued together again. In the margin, on the bottom, in large, shaky letters was written the word: "Please!" I wasn't bothered again. It was after this that I began to wonder: If they're *that* unformidable, why bother to fight back? (PATSY *stirs*) It's very dangerous to challenge a system unless you're completely at peace with the thought that you're not going to miss it when it collapses. Patsy— You can't be the one to change. (PATSY *stares, uncomprehending*) I'm the one who has to change.

PATSY (*Tired*)   Alfred, what are you talking about?

ALFRED   When I first met you I remember thinking, this is the most formidable person I have ever known. I don't stand a chance! I'll try to stay the way I am. I'll try desperately! (*Happily*) But I don't stand a chance! It's only a matter of time. Very soon now I'll be (*Smiles*) —different. I'll be able to look at half-empty glasses of water and say, This glass isn't half empty. This glass is half *full!* You can't be the one to sell out. *I* was supposed to sell out. (*Stares miserably at the disheveled, slumped-over* PATSY *he's created*) Why doesn't somebody beat me up now? (*Starts off*) I'm going out to Central Park!
    (*He exits*)

PATSY (*Watches him go. Slowly straightens*)   Alfred— Come back here! (*A long pause, then* ALFRED *enters, uncertain*) You see what happens when you start fooling around with the rules? (*Recovering, holds out her arms*) It begins with weddings and it ends with—well, there's no telling where it ends. (*More affirmative*) There are reasons for doing things the old way. (*With growing assurance she takes his hands*) Don't look for trouble and trouble won't look for you. (*Very strong*) I don't say there aren't problems but you have to fight. You are going to fight. (*Squeezes her arms around him*) Starting now. Is that right? (*Pause. Finally he nods*) And you are going to feel. Starting right now. Is that right? (*Pause. He finally nods*) I don't want a nod. I want an answer. Say, "Yes, Patsy."

ALFRED   Yes, Patsy.

PATSY   Yes, Patsy, what?

ALFRED   Yes, Patsy—I'm going to feel.

PATSY   Starting when?

ALFRED   Starting as soon as I can manage it.

PATSY   Starting *when*?

ALFRED   Starting now.

PATSY   And what's your first feeling?

ALFRED   It's sort of distant.

PATSY Don't be ashamed of it.

ALFRED It's worship.

PATSY Of God?

ALFRED Of you.

PATSY You're doing fine. (*Kisses him. Puts her arms around him*) My lover. (*Kisses him*) My hero! (*Kisses him.* ALFRED *tentatively responds. Embrace builds.* CAROL *and* MARJORIE *enter. React with warm surprise. They put their arms around each other*)

MARJORIE Aren't they an attractive couple?
(*Sound of gunshot. Window shatters. Explosion of blood as* PATSY'S *hand flies up to her head. She drops.* CAROL *and* MARJORIE *freeze.* ALFRED *stares down at* PATSY, *then melting into his daydream pose, slowly turns away. The street noise is loud through the shattered window*)

Blackout

The Newquist apartment, six months later. There have been changes. Heavy blackout drapes cover the windows. Large photographic blowups of PATSY's eyes, nose, hair, smiling lips and teeth are hung unframed on the walls, and are in evidence in several two- and three-foot high stacks on the floor. (These pictures can be premounted on the reverse sides of the molded sections of the walls and pivoted about during the scene change.)

ALFRED is bent over a small photo stand, shooting away with a camera, humming to himself. He looks happy. Sporadic gunfire is heard in the background. He pays no attention. Doorbell. ALFRED takes a quick last look at the work on the stand, goes to the door, detouring past the couch to pick up a long cardboard carton and shove it out of sight under the couch. He has the beginnings of a black eye.

ALFRED   One minute. (He checks through keyhole and unlocks door. There are now four different kinds of locks and bolts on door, including a police bar) One more minute. (Opens door) Hi, Dad!

CAROL (Enters carrying bulging brief case)   It's murder out there.

(ALFRED *tries to relieve him of brief case.* CAROL
brusquely pushes him aside)

ALFRED   Hey, Dad, you're limping!

CAROL (*Shouts*)   How many times have I told you not to
call me Dad!

ALFRED   I can't call you "Dad." I can't call you "Carol."
What can I call you? "Dear"?
        (*Long exchange of stares,* ALFRED'S *good-humored,*
        CAROL'S *sullen*)

CAROL   Call me "Mr. Newquist."

ALFRED   You're just in a bad mood, Dad. Let me fix you
a drink.
        (*Crosses to bar*)

CAROL (*Sits*)   I don't want you to fix me— Bourbon.

ALFRED (*Serving drink*)   The family that drinks together
sinks together.

CAROL (*Drinks*)   Maybe I'd feel better if you turned on
the air conditioner. It blots out the sound of the shooting. Agh, the hell with it. It's here to stay. I might as
well get used to it. (*Conspiratorial*) I dropped by police
headquarters this afternoon. That's why I'm late.

ALFRED   Are you late?

CAROL (*Annoyed*)   *Yes, I'm late!* I'm four hours late. I told you I'd be finished with my deliveries at one. Any calls?

ALFRED   The Breather, once or twice. He's picking up the pace again.

CAROL (*Mutters*)   Asthmatic bastard!

ALFRED   I never told you, but the day after Patsy died he rang up. I went a little crazy—I started screaming, "Didn't you hear the news? No need to call any more! Patsy's dead!" In no more than ten seconds, he called back. And he *spoke!* He said, "I don't know what to say. I'm terribly sorry." And then before hanging up he said, "What can we do? The world's gone crazy!" Not another breath out of him until this week. In mourning, I suppose.

CAROL   You sure it's the same one?

ALFRED   You think we're on a mailing list? God, I *hope* it's the same one.

CAROL   This damned business! (*Conspiratorial*) Keep this under your hat—but I paid an unexpected call on police headquarters this afternoon.

ALFRED   I'm surprised they didn't shoot you.

CAROL   They did shoot me. (*Rubs his leg*) It was my own damned fault. I didn't give the password. (*Hands empty glass to* ALFRED, *who pours drink*) I feel sorry for those poor bastards. I know a lot of them by their first names. I call them Jimmy, and Mac and Phil. They call me Carol. (*Quickly*) It sounds different when *they* say it. I had a fifteen-minute talk with Lieutenant Practice. Busy as hell but he found fifteen minutes to talk to me. He's convinced they're closing in on the conspiracy.

ALFRED   What conspiracy?

CAROL   Three hundred and forty-five unsolved murders in six months. There's got to be a conspiracy! (ALFRED *shrugs*) There's *got* to be some logic behind all this. Any other calls?

ALFRED   You mean orders? No.

CAROL   I have to admit to you these new pictures are really catching on! Fifty orders of Patsy Number Seven last week, ten orders so far this week of Patsy Number Eight and Fifteen, and five orders from an uptown gallery for the entire Patsy series. (*Thickly*) We wouldn't have come through this without you, Alfred.

ALFRED (*Shrugs*)   I had to do *something* after I abandoned my shit series.

CAROL (*Emotional*) But you didn't have to put *me* to work. Nobody asked. (*Suddenly defensive*) I didn't ask—

ALFRED You're a top-notch salesman, Dad.

CAROL I'm an order taker and a messenger boy. But when I get back on my feet—

ALFRED It'll be no time.

CAROL Who knows if they'll even want me back at the office. Six months— (*Shakes his head*) You've been very good—to us.

ALFRED Forget it.

CAROL (*Nods*) I'll do that. (*A pained sigh*) I wish I resented you less.

ALFRED Keep up the fight, tiger.

CAROL (*Sadly*) Patsy used to call me tiger. Everything you say these days reminds me of Patsy.

ALFRED (*Thoughtful, a little sad*) I owe Patsy a lot. (*Cheerful again*) Why shouldn't I talk like her?

CAROL Just as long as you don't dress like her. Where's Kenny?

ALFRED   In her closet.

CAROL   Little son of a bitch! Christ, I hope it's only a phase. I don't see where that Doctor Harm is helping any—

ALFRED   Doctor Good.

CAROL   Yeah? Well, I suppose he must be good. Otherwise he'd take a hell of a kidding. (*Depressed*) Agh—I don't understand anything any more. You know how I get through the day?—don't say a word of this to Marjorie— in planned segments. I get up in the morning and I think, Okay, a sniper didn't get me for breakfast, let's see if I can go for my morning walk without being mugged. Okay, I finished my walk, let's see if I can make it back home without having a brick dropped on my head from the top of a building. Okay, I'm safe in the lobby, let's see if I can go up in the elevator without getting a knife in my ribs. Okay, I made it to the front door, let's see if I can open it without finding burglars in the hall. Okay, I made it to the hall, let's see if I can walk into the living room and not find the rest of my family dead. *This Goddamned city!*

ALFRED (*With sympathy*)   Got to fight, tiger.

CAROL   You do enough fighting for one family. Where'd you get that eye?
    (*He indicates* ALFRED's *mouse*)

ALFRED   Some kid was staring at me in the park. I hit him.

CAROL (*Tired*)   Another fight?

ALFRED   What could I do? The little bastard was *staring* at me! (CAROL *turns away in disgust. Placating*) I beat the crap out of him—(CAROL *reluctantly smiles.* ALFRED *starts to spar with him*) Let's go a couple of quick ones, tiger.

CAROL (*Retreating*)   Come on. Cut it out. Cut it out.

ALFRED (*Sparring*)   Pow! Pow! Pow! Boy if Patsy could have only been there! (*Mimes a wicked kick*) And she said I didn't feel. Every time I get into one of these things, I think of her—I think of her alive and me coming home weary, every night—you know, after I beat somebody up, and she meets me at the door, looking up at me with eyes full of pride, and she takes my swollen fists in her hands, and she kisses my knuckles—what a dream. Why is it we only learn when it's too late? (*Spars*) Pow! Pow! It was my fourth fight this week. I suppose all that euphoria takes something out of you. Anyhow, I got very faint, so I sat down on a park bench to rest—and I found *this* lying there.
        (*He holds up the* Daily News)

CAROL (*Reading*)   "Hippie Minister Slain at Church Happening." They're sure giving that son of a bitch a hell of a lot of free publicity!

89

ALFRED It wasn't so much the story that interested me. I don't have the patience for facts, or any of that nonsense any more. What interested me was (*Shows* CAROL *newspaper*) this photograph of the body—what does it look like?

CAROL That son of a bitch. With his eyes closed.

ALFRED (*Excited*) No! Look closer!
    (*He raises newspaper to* CAROL's *face*)

CAROL What do I want to look for? This is the silliest—

ALFRED Don't you see the dots?

CAROL What dots?

ALFRED Here! The little black dots that make up the photograph. Use your eyes, Dad!

CAROL (*Pushes paper away*) Okay. I see them! So what!

ALFRED Keep staring at them. (*Raises paper closer to* CAROL's *face*) You see how they slowly begin to move? (*Takes paper away from* CAROL) I was sitting on the park bench looking at this photograph of the body and the little black dots began to break apart—they began detaching themselves from the body—the dots that make up his eyes—the little black dots that make up his mouth —and the top of his head—they just lifted off his body— and broke apart. Until it wasn't the body of Henry Dupas I was staring at, but millions of little black dots coming at me until I thought I was going to be sucked in alive. I panicked! I wanted to close off! But then I thought, Wait a minute, that's the *old* you, the *pre-Patsy* you. So I let go and I was swallowed. Into a free-floating constellation of dots. Fantastic! I swung my eyes away from the photograph—I looked up at a tree. Do you know how many trillions of dots there are in one Central Park tree? And then the dots that made up the tree merged with the dots that made up the sky merged with the dots that made up the park bench and the grass and the dirt path and the three colored kids walking toward me carrying bicycle chains. Do you know the wild arrangement of dots that's made every time you punch somebody out? Those poor kids must've thought I was crazy —humming as I beat their heads against the sidewalk. (*Offstage muffled shot*) I've been studying this newspaper for hours now trying to figure out a way of decomposing everything into dots.

CAROL   I don't know why you want to fool around. We're doing *extremely* well with our current line.

ALFRED   There gets to be something ultimately stifling about taking photographs of old photographs.

CAROL (*Reasonably*)   You enlarge them.

ALFRED   It's limited! I want to do *life*! If I could somehow
make people see themselves as trillions upon trillions of
free-wheeling, interchanging dots—(*Loses himself in
thought.* CAROL *shakes his head, says nothing. Doorbell.* ALFRED *puts an arm on* CAROL's *shoulder and
goes to door*) One minute. (*Looks through peephole.
Begins the process of unlocking the door*) One more
minute.

MARJORIE   (*Enters, flushed, carrying leaking shopping bag*)
Will you look at this mess? They shot a hole in my
shopping bag.

CAROL   (*Stricken*)   You could have been killed!

MARJORIE   (*Annoyed*)   I get shot at every day. We all do,
Carol. Don't make more of it than it is. (*To* ALFRED) I
saw that nice Lieutenant Practice in the lobby. He looks
simply awful. I invited him up for coffee just as soon as
he gets finished investigating the new murder.

CAROL   What new murder?

MARJORIE   (*Bored*)   I don't know. It's in the other wing.
(ALFRED *reaches under couch and slides out long
carton he concealed at start of scene. It is not the
box he intended to pull out. He slides it back and
reaches for a smaller box, which he hands to*
MARJORIE)

ALFRED   Mom.

MARJORIE (*Opens box*) Alfred. Oh, Alfred! (*Removes flowers*) Aren't they beautiful! Look, Carol, they're flowers! (*Clutches them to her. Cries*) I'm sorry—there is so little thought left of giving today that I've forgotten how to receive. (*Drops flowers. Rushes offstage, holding her hands to her face. Offstage*) Kenny! Let me in there!

> (*Offstage toilet flush, door slams.* KENNY *camps in, wearing dark glasses, carrying* Vogue. CAROL, *who cannot look at him, exits.* KENNY *sees flowers on floor. He picks them up*)

ALFRED You want 'em?

KENNY (*Drops flowers*) What do I want with your fruity flowers?

> (ALFRED *returns to camera stand.* MARJORIE *enters*)

MARJORIE (*Staring down at flowers*) Alfred, you are a love. (ALFRED, *distracted, waves from camera stand*) When I was twelve-and-a-half my mother and father would cart the whole pack of us out to the country and we would always picnic near the flowers. There were so many more flowers in those days. We'd pick every last one and bring it back to the city. (*To* KENNY *as she stoops for flowers*) No one does the cleaning up around here except me. (*Doorbell.* KENNY *starts for door*) I'll get it. (KENNY *spots protruding edge of the carton under the couch*) Who is it? Will you step a little closer and turn your face into the light please?

(*She checks peephole, starts to unlock door.* KENNY *slides out carton, is about to lift lid*)

ALFRED (*Still peering into camera on stand*) That's—not—a—good—idea—

KENNY (*Whirls*) Who died and made you boss? (*Shot splinters window near* KENNY's *head just as* LIEUTENANT PRACTICE *enters.* KENNY *shakes fist at window, screams*) Fags!

MARJORIE (*To* PRACTICE) You'll have to pardon the mess.

CAROL (*Enters, glances over to* KENNY *at window, hurries over to* PRACTICE, *shakes his hand*) Well, well, well. This is an unexpected pleasure. Alfred, look who's decided to pay us a visit. Lieutenant Practice! (ALFRED, *at work, gives a perfunctory wave of hand.* CAROL *whispers*) He's working. Goes on day and night. It's no accident he's successful.

PRACTICE And I'm not. Is that it?

CAROL (*Takes his arm*) I didn't mean that. You're making great strides. Nobody expects very much anyway. (PRACTICE *draws arm away*) Nobody's complaining.

MARJORIE (*Cheerful*) We certainly haven't complained. And if anyone has a right to—

PRACTICE (*Sad*) Can I please have a glass of milk, Mrs. Newquist?

(*He sits down*)

MARJORIE Of course, dear.

PRACTICE And a cookie. Jeez, I'm depressed. There's got to be some logical explanation to all of this.

(MARJORIE *exits*)

CAROL You've got nothing to be ashamed of. You'll figure it out.

PRACTICE (*Hands* CAROL *envelope*) I really stopped by to return this. I don't know what got into me this afternoon.

CAROL (*Looks nervously around*) It's all right. It's yours! Forget it!

PRACTICE I *can't* accept a $250 check. I know your heart was in the right place, Mr. Newquist, but believe me, it's not gonna make us find your daughter's murderer any quicker.

CAROL Keep it! Keep it! You never can tell—

MARJORIE (*Enters with glass of milk*) Drink this. You'll

feel better. Carol, are you giving money away again? You know, Lieutenant, every time we pass a policeman he hands him five dollars.

CAROL   I just want the boys on the beat to know somebody still has faith in them.

PRACTICE   (*Drinks*)   I needed this. (ALFRED *slides carton back under couch;* KENNY *watches with interest.* PRACTICE *examines hand holding glass. It has a tremor*) I wasn't like this when I met you six months ago, was I? Wasn't I a lot more self-confident? Jeez, the way I used to enter the scene of a crime! Like I owned the Goddamned world! Can you put a little Scotch in this milk, please? And a piece of cheese on this cookie? There's going to be a shakeup, you know. When there are three hundred and forty-five murders and none of them get solved. (*Angry*) *Somebody has to be elected fall guy!* (*Accepts drink*) Thank you. Maybe a piece of ice like a good fellow. (*Hands drink back*) Somewhere there's a logical pattern to this whole business. There *has* to be. (*Accepts cookie*) I didn't ask for butter on the cookie, just cheese. (*Hands cookie back*) Thank you. And these damned vigilante groups —they're not helping matters. Black against white. White against black. What ever became of human dignity? (*Accepts drink*) Oh, for Christ sakes, only *one* piece of ice? Let's get it right, huh? Say, what kind of cheese is this? Sharp cheddar? You ought to know by now with my stomach I can't take sharp cheddar! Come on! *Will you shape up?* (*Reflective*) Sooner or later there's a pattern. Sooner or later everything falls into place. I believe that. If I didn't believe that I wouldn't want to wake up to see the sun tomorrow morning. (CAROL *and* MARJORIE *scrambling from different directions with drink and cheese*) Is *this* what I asked for? Goddamnit, *I want some cooperation!* (*A shot—milk glass explodes in his hand. All except* PRACTICE *stare toward window. He stares at remnant of glass in his hand*) Every crime has its own pattern of logic. Everything has an order. If we can't find that order it's not because it doesn't exist, but only because we've incorrectly observed some vital piece of evidence. Let us examine the evidence. (*Places glass in handkerchief, handkerchief in pocket*) Number one. In the last six months three hundred and forty-five homicides have been committed in this city. The victims have ranged variously in sex, age, social status and color. Number two. In none of the three hundred and forty-five homicides have we been able to establish motive. Number three. All three hundred and forty-five homicides remain listed on our books as unsolved. So much for the evidence. A subtle pattern begins to emerge. What is this pattern? What is it that each of these three hundred and forty-five homicides have in common? They have in common three things: a) that they have nothing in common; b) that they have no motive; c) that, consequently, they remain unsolved. The pattern becomes clearer. Orthodox police procedure dictates that the basic question you ask in all such investigations is: 1) who has the most to gain? What could possibly be the single unifying motive behind three hundred and forty-five un-connected homicides? When a case does not gel it is often not because we lack the necessary facts, but because we have observed our facts incorrectly. In each of these three hundred and forty-five homicides we observed our facts incorrectly. Following normal routine we looked for a cause. And we could find no cause. Had we looked for effect we would have had our answer that much sooner. What is the effect of three hundred and forty-five unsolved homicide cases? The effect is loss of faith in law-enforcement personnel. That is our motive. The pattern is complete. We are involved here in a far-reaching conspiracy to undermine respect for our basic beliefs and most sacred institutions. Who is behind this conspiracy? Once again ask the question: Who has the most to gain? People in high places. Their names would astound you. People in low places. Concealing their activities beneath a cloak of poverty. People in all walks of life. Left wing and right wing. Black and white. Students and scholars. A conspiracy of such ominous proportions that we may not know the whole truth in our lifetime, and we will never be able to reveal all the facts. We are readying mass arrests. (*Rises to leave*) I'm going to try my best to see that you people get every possible break. If there is any information you wish to volunteer at this time it will be held in the strictest confidence. (*Waits for response. There is none. Crosses to door and opens it*) I strongly advise against any of you trying to leave town.

 (*Quickly exits*)

CAROL (*Gradually exploding*)   What's left? What's there
left? I'm a reasonable man. Just explain to me what I
have left to believe in. I swear to God the tide's rising!
Two hundred and fifty dollars. Gimme, gimme. We need
honest cops! People just aren't being protected any more!
We need a revival of honor. And trust! We need the
Army! We need a giant fence around every block in the
city. An electrically charged fence. And everyone who
wants to leave the block has to have a pass. And a hair-
cut. And can't talk with a filthy mouth! We need respect
for a man's reputation. TV cameras! That's what we
need! In every building lobby, in every elevator, in every
apartment, in every room. Public servants who *are* public
servants! And if they catch you doing anything funny
—to yourself, or anybody—they break down the door and
beat the living— A return to common sense! We have to
have lobotomies for anyone who earns less than ten
thousand a year. I don't like it but it's an emergency. Our
side needs weapons too. Is it fair that they should have
all the weapons? We've got to train ourselves! And steel
ourselves! It's freedom I'm talking about! There's a fox
loose in the chicken coop! *Kill him!* I want my *freedom!*
   (*He collapses*)

ALFRED   Let's get him inside.
      (ALFRED *and* MARJORIE *carry* CAROL *off*. KENNY
      *watches after them, quickly crosses to box, slides
      it out and lifts lid as* MARJORIE *enters.* KENNY *slams
      down lid.* MARJORIE *grabs bottle from bar and exits.*
      KENNY *lifts rifle out of box, goes to window, parts*

*curtain slightly, aims—*ALFRED *enters.* KENNY, *startled, holds rifle out to him*)

KENNY   I thought it was more flowers.

ALFRED   Use it.

KENNY   What do I want to use it for? I've only been in analysis four months. I've never fired one of these in my life.

ALFRED   Me too.

KENNY (*Suspicious*)   Why'd you get it?

ALFRED (*Shrugs*)   It was on sale. (*Stares at rifle in* KENNY'*s hands. Goes to door, relocks it. To* KENNY) Put it away—(KENNY *begins to*) No. (ALFRED *crosses to* KENNY, *takes rifle, studies it*) You notice, if you stare at it long enough it breaks into dots?

KENNY (*Studies rifle*)   No—

ALFRED (*Turns rifle in his hand*)   Trillions of dots— (*Pulls trigger. A loud click*) It's not loaded.
     (*Puts it down*)

KENNY   Why don't you load it?

ALFRED   I don't know how.
     (*Hands rifle to* KENNY, *who backs away from it*)

KENNY (*Shakes his head*) The Army rejected me four times. The fifth time they said if I ever came around again they'd have me arrested. (*Reaches into box. Takes out instruction booklet, turns page, reads*) "Nomenclature." (*Turns page*) "Trigger housing group." (*Turns page*) "To load: hold the weapon by the forearm of the stock with left hand. Rotate the safety to its 'on' position. Lock the bolt open. With right hand insert the magazine into the magazine opening and push up."

MARJORIE (*Enters. Looks over* ALFRED's *shoulder as he struggles to insert magazine clip*) I don't know about these things, dear, but I found the best way to deal with the unfamiliar is to think things back to their source. (*She takes rifle out of his hands*) Now, it would seem to me that *this* goes in—(*Struggles.* CAROL *enters. Observes*) Damn it! They must have given you the wrong—(CAROL *takes rifle out of her hands, expertly loads it, tosses it to* ALFRED. MARJORIE *is very impressed*) Dear!

ALFRED (*Hands rifle back to* CAROL) Go on, Dad. You loaded it. You go first.

CAROL (*Solemnly hands rifle back*) It's yours.

KENNY Where'd you learn that, Dad? It's a trick, right?
(CAROL *stares scornfully at* KENNY, *takes rifle.* ALFRED *parts curtains*)

ALFRED Can you see well enough?
(CAROL *aims, fires*)

KENNY   I think you got somebody.

MARJORIE   Let me see! I never can see! (ALFRED *boosts her*) Yes! Yes! Somebody's lying there!

CAROL (*To* ALFRED)   Why don't you try *your* luck? (*Hands over rifle*)

ALFRED (*Hands rifle to* KENNY)   You first, Kenny.

KENNY   Gee.

ALFRED (*Reassuring*)   I'll go right after you.
          (KENNY *quickly gets up with rifle. Fires out window*)

CAROL   Miss!

KENNY   You made me nervous! You were *looking!*

CAROL (*Takes rifle*)   It's Alfred's turn.

KENNY   No fair! You shook my arm.

ALFRED   Let him have another shot.
          (KENNY *aims carefully, fires*)

CAROL (*Looking into street. Very proud*)   Son of a bitch!

MARJORIE (*Hugs him*)   You did it! You did it!
          (CAROL *reloads, hands rifle to* ALFRED)

KENNY (*Cool, manly*)   Dad and I got *our* two.
(CAROL *puts his arm around* KENNY'*s shoulder.*
ALFRED *aims out window, fires*)

CAROL   You know who I think he got?

MARJORIE   Lieutenant Practice!
(*All jump up and down in self-congratulations—
ad lib shouts, Texas yells.* ALFRED, CAROL *and* KENNY
in unison; none of the following is intelligible)

ALFRED   Fantastic! What a picture! Unbelievable! Fantastic! What a picture!

CAROL   Some hell of a team, eh, boys! Now we're moving!
Now we'll show 'em! Show the whole Goddamn world!

KENNY   Son of a bitch! Bastard! See me, Dad? Goddamn!
Son of a bitch! Goddamn! See me, Alfred?
(*During all of this* MARJORIE *has made a sprightly
exit, instantly reentering, wheeling serving cart.
She lights candles on dining-room table*)

MARJORIE   Come an' git it!
(*The others, wrestling, horsing around, move slowly
toward table*)

MARJORIE   Boys!
(*Amidst great noise, bustle, serving of drinks, they
finally sit. More ad lib cries, friendly shoving*)

ALFRED (*Over the others*) Hey, how about Mom trying her luck after dinner?
(*Cheers, ad lib agreement*)

MARJORIE (*Serving*) It's so nice to have my family laughing again. You know, for a while I was really worried.
(*General merriment*)

Curtain

Production Notes

The two letters below were written in February and April of 1967 to Christopher Morahan, the director of The Royal Shakespeare Company's production of *Little Murders*. The London version of the play began rehearsals two weeks after the New York opening (one and a half weeks after the New York closing), barely leaving time for a good depression.

February 1, 1967

Dear Chris:

I've started this letter twice but a pre-production torpor has fallen over me (we go into rehearsals here on Friday), and I find it almost impossible to do anything, including the cartoon—which is inconvenient because it is my livelihood.

Let me answer your letter point by point. Absolutely right on the style being naturalistic, with the mutually understood reservation that once having found the reality in their characters, the actors will be absolutely hilarious.*

The play is a post-assassination play, but the era of

---

* Absolute nonsense. The play was given a considerably more stylized production in London, and played remarkably better than it did in New York. This has convinced me of nothing other than that the author, while always correct in his intentions, is sometimes mistaken about the means to fulfill them.

gratuitous violence that Kennedy's death highlighted was, I think, coming into its own before November 22, 1963. It grows out of the frustrations of a previously isolationist nation having to go internationalist in an immense way, feeling unappreciated, unloved, and finally unwanted for all its good works and, in reaction, turning narcissistically violent toward the outside world (Santo Domingo, Vietnam) and paranoiacally violent toward its own internal world (race violence, random violence, motiveless mass murders). All of this the heritage of a Cold War that has taught us that power not only corrupts, it also disables, and that one American is no longer worth ten of the enemy (the previously accepted ratio), but rather that in guerrilla war eight Americans are worth one Viet Cong. A trying time.

Into this atmosphere steps Patsy Newquist, the all-American girl, Doris Day of ten years ago—a tomboy as a kid, a cheerleader, a gold-cup winner on the school swimming team, the most popular girl in the class, the pride of her family, the child of the West who finds all dreams attainable if one just has the get up and go. She has spirit, exuberance, great feminine strength and an indomitable spirit, all of which implies that she's oblivious to the lessons of anyone else's life but her own. But she is likeable, as are the rest of the family, in their own ways. She is not by choice a castrator, and it gives her no pleasure to bend men to her will. But if there's one thing she knows (and self-doubt has never touched her), it is that she is right and *they* are wrong—and therefore they must *change!* She believes in initiative, resourcefulness, home, the family, God, motherhood, and country. But, as she tells her father, years of relentless triumph are beginning to take their toll, and she sees Alfred as her last chance. He is not one of the effete, manageable but unmarriageable men of her past, but a huge, somewhat slovenly heterosexual who, once he is given the right slant on life, will be absolutely ideal. Patsy is, or should be, that movie myth, the girl next door—slightly over the hill but still damned attractive. She, of all of them, must be real (even at the expense of laughs, though I think she can get both). If she is played as a figure of mockery it is unimportant that she dies. But in the proper context, when she is killed, it is the winner dying, it is optimism, the positive values, old-fashioned horse sense, logic, happiness, security, the home, and John F. Kennedy.

Alfred is her opposite number. Things have come hard for him. He is not an automatic winner. He has been in the middle or at the bottom often enough to form attitudes that allow him to survive either defeat or triumph. He has detached himself from all emotional involvement: he doesn't know what love is, and he doesn't know what violence is. He simply stands there and allows both to strike him.

If Patsy had lived he would have made, as he promises her, some effort to change. But not enough. He would go through periods of acceptance and withdrawal. And finally Patsy would lie punch-drunk, a victim of her own exhausted and pointless idealism. Alfred would indeed be changed —no longer taking pictures of shit, no longer taking pictures of anything. Patsy would support both of them until Alfred

would one day disappear. But Patsy is shot. And shot at
the very moment that Alfred sees for the first time since his
childhood the possibilities that he has so long denied himself: the possibilities of hope, of idealism, of a soul saved
from the brink by romantic love and womanly guidance.
And this is a loss he cannot accept. Patsy's death is one
thing, but the death of the reawakened dream she symbol-
ized to him is another matter altogether. So despite the
evidence of her shattered philosophy lying at his feet, he
must tell himself that he was wrong and that she was right.
Life is not shit. Life can be beautiful. Patsy's death, then,
becomes his triumph, his test, he will make her proud of
him by becoming her: filling her role with the family,
turning optimistic, taking charge. In his mind he has opted
for health. He has not the slightest inkling that he has
gone mad. (This last business I have tried to clarify in a
new speech in Act Two, Scene Two, that you will receive
shortly, along with other revisions.)

The Judge and Lieutenant Practice are Carol's repre-
sentatives: Alfred, the outsider, who takes pictures of shit
and does not want God in the ceremony, is breaking down
the order of Carol's life, and some sense must be brought
back into it. The Judge provides the solid sense of tradition
and authority; Practice, the declining sense of law and
order. Practice is Carol's last hold on the old world, split
once by the murder of Steve, shattered again by Patsy's
murder. Now he is holding on for dear life to that last of
all authority figures for threatened members of the middle
class: the cop. So Practice is there to show to Carol that

even this last mythic semblance of order has broken down. At which point he falls apart.

Dupas should, I think, be played young (Alfred's age) and in clerical garb, with the addition of motorcycle boots. He speaks quietly, unsensationally—as would a patient teacher explaining to a slightly backward class what he knows to be perfectly obvious.

The blackouts in New York occur normally by blocks, very occasionally by districts, and, so far, only once by an entire seaboard. When the lights fail in the Newquist apartment they should also fail in whatever other windows are visible in the general area.

I should have a new script to you within a week. (It's mostly tidying up, no major revisions except for the shift in locales for the Judge's scene.)

Best regards,
Jules

April 28, 1967

Dear Chris:

I appreciate your being so understanding about my long delay in writing. We opened Tuesday, we close Saturday and I am, for the moment, convinced that *Little Murders* was an English play all along. The Boston critics who didn't understand it understood it better than the New York critics who totally withdrew from it, followed immediately thereafter by the audience. My dismay has been replaced by hostility, so I am back to normal.

The Judge's scene, as rumored, has been cut.* The only other major alteration is the Practice scene, where I have changed the murder case to one more closely connected to the theme of paranoia and random violence. I have also made some trims in the scene between Carol and Alfred.

Our most serious problem was preparing the audience for the shift from family comedy in Act One (ending with the wedding riot) to the more serious comment in Act Two. The single insight I have brought out of two months of production is that if the actors play the jokes (as they were too inclined to do here) and not the family relationships with all their underlying tensions, we have an audience so very happy at the end of Act One that they are thrown into confusion by the rest of the play. I don't mean that the first scene should not be funny, or that venom need be added to the performances; it should not. I only mean that we must communicate authentic family tensions as an underpinning for the laughs. I think even more than the external sounds of violence that this is necessary to set the mood of the evening. It seems to me that Marjorie is the key here. If she is played as the traditional scatterbrained theatrical stereotype, we are lost. Underneath her surface gabbiness, coquettishness and self-pity there is a visible strain of barely contained hysteria. It is she who sets the family's pace. Alfred's pace is very different.

We should not tip our hand by allowing a fey Kenny in the early scenes. At this point he is not effete, but neuter, masking his desire to be a woman (to be Patsy, really: to him the most masculine image in the family) by

* This scene was restored for the London and all other productions.

a shrewdly constructed clownishness. His running off in Patsy's heels is not camp, however. He simply got caught, that's all.

Other problems: making Patsy's breakdown not repellent to the audience as it was, in too many instances, in this production. We must like her, even in her absurdity and hysteria, or her sudden death will be good news, not bad. I've had to tone down the scene slightly, but whether this is due to a weakness of script or performance I cannot, at the moment, say. For the present at least I would prefer going with the original version. Barbara Jefford sounds marvelous. (When we were casting Patsy I looked at some American Portias, but, alas . . .)

The sound-and-light montage has reduced itself to a sound montage, and in its present form adds little, if anything. The stop-motion idea was never truly tried—and I am not sure, at this point, that it has any value. The way we go up now is on the empty set, dark, street sounds from the window. A toilet flush, Kenny exits from the bathroom, pistol shots from the window. He takes a step toward them, the door unlocks, he dashes back to the bathroom and Marjorie enters.

Our set, as it turns out, was overly naturalistic (the author's idea); yours sounds better. The more we can do in set and sound to indicate the vulnerability of the household, the better off we will be for the violence that comes later.

You will have a revised script by the middle of next week. I arrive Sunday night, May 7th.

Best,
Jules

NOTES FOR THE OPENING OF A PLAY ENTITLED AUTHOR IMMEDIATELY PRIOR TO PERFORM FRIENDS, RELATIVES, BIOGRAPHERS AND

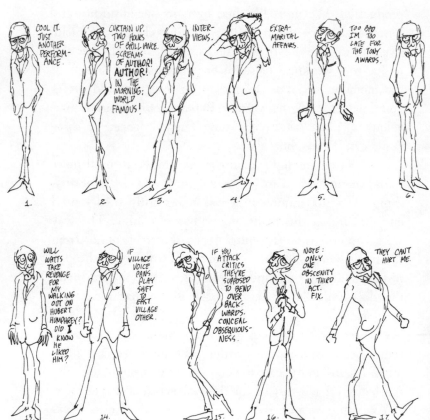

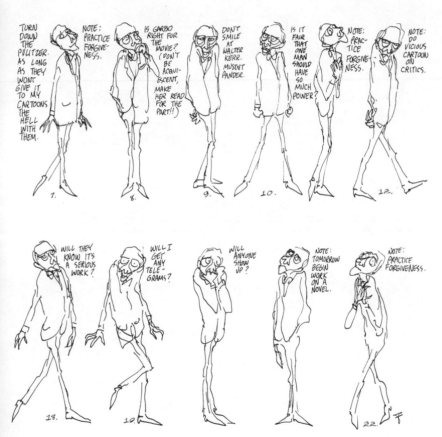

ABOUT THE AUTHOR

JULES FEIFFER's work now appears in more than one hundred and fifteen publications here and abroad. He has published ten collections of cartoons, including *Feiffer's Marriage Manual* and a novel, *Harry, the Rat with Women.* His new play, *God Bless,* is being produced at the Yale Drama School, by Mark Taper Forum and by The Royal Shakespeare Company of London, in the fall of 1968; it will also be seen off-Broadway in January 1969.